Collins

Social Studies
Atlas
for Jamaica

PRIMARY
WORKBOOK

Series editor: Farah Christian

William Collins' dream of knowledge for all began with the publication of his first book in 1819. A self-educated mill worker, he not only enriched millions of lives, but also founded a flourishing publishing house. Today, staying true to this spirit, Collins books are packed with inspiration, innovation and practical expertise. They place you at the centre of a world of possibility and give you exactly what you need to explore it.

Collins. Freedom to teach.

Published by Collins
An imprint of HarperCollins*Publishers*
Westerhill Road, Bishopbriggs, Glasgow, G64 2QT

HarperCollins Publishers
Macken House, 39/40 Mayor Street Upper, Dublin 1, D01 C9W8, Ireland

Browse the complete Collins Caribbean catalogue at
www.collins.co.uk/caribbeanschools

10 9 8

ISBN 9780008300241

British Library Cataloguing in Publication Data
A catalogue record for this publication is available from the British Library.

The publishers gratefully acknowledge the permission granted to reproduce the copyright material in this book. Every effort has been made to trace copyright holders and to obtain their permission for the use of copyright material. The publishers will gladly receive any information enabling them to rectify any error or omission at the first opportunity.

Series editor: Farah Christian
Author: Naam Thomas
Publisher: Elaine Higgleton
Project manager: Rachel Allegro
Copy editor: Bruce Nicholson
Proofreader: Louise Robb
Typesetter: QBS
Cover image: Photo Spirit/Shutterstock; Danita Delmont/Shutterstock
Printed in United Kingdom

Acknowledgements
p44(t) Art Directors & TRIP/Alamy Stock Photo; **p44(b)** Robin Moore/Getty Images; **p47** Robert Fried/Alamy Stock Photo; **p70** Vladimir Kanuh/Shutterstock

Contents

Introduction

This *Collins Jamaica Atlas for Social Studies Workbook* has been specially written to complement the *Collins Social Studies Atlas for Jamaica*. It contains activities that have been developed to meet the learning objectives relating to Jamaica and its geography, history, heritage, land use, environment and government in grades 4–6 of the National Standards Curriculum for Social Studies.

This workbook contains activities that will require students to apply what they learn, and also to analyze data and to make deductive reasoning using the contents of the atlas, in line with the objectives of the curriculum. Some of the activities include students analyzing and interpreting map information, analyzing and creating statistical graphs and diagrams, drawing conclusions from maps and timelines, and writing summaries. Importantly, many of the activities in this workbook provide practice of the skills – such as using data presented to answer a specific question, extrapolating key information from that data, and explaining how the data helps to answer the question – that students need for the new **Curriculum Based Test** of the **PEP**.

We have also included activities that bring in **STEM** and **Extended Learning**:

- The **STEM activities** are ideas for projects that are designed to help students learn to apply scientific and mathematical principles to problems while using a range of tools, including digital resources. Through these activities, students will practise problem-solving and reflection on tasks completed.

- **Extended Learning activities** are designed to help students move beyond the atlas to explore other sources of information. These activities will create opportunities for students to carry out further research and to use a range of resources to gather information to complete the tasks. These activities cannot be directly completed using the atlas alone. However, they are tied directly to the curriculum units and may be assigned to students as homework.

Some activities related to vocabulary require the student to use the *Collins Jamaican School Dictionary*. If this dictionary is unavailable, any good dictionary may be used instead.

In some cases, we suggest that students carry out research online, and suggest some websites that students could use. Please make sure that all internet-based research is supervised to ensure that students are only accessing relevant sites, that students are only using the internet for research purposes and not for social media and emails, and to make sure that students are not in any way exposing themselves to risk. Please make sure that any internet-based research carried out in school is in line with school policy, and please encourage parents to supervise any internet-based research that is set as homework.

Grade 4 – Term 1, Unit 1

> The English-speaking Caribbean is home to many groups of people. A group of people who have a similar history and culture is called an *ethnic group*. To learn more about an ethnic group, we can study the country where they came from. This is called their *ethnic origin*. The first group of people to settle in Jamaica were the Tainos and for a long time they were the only ethnic group on the island.

1 Look at pages 20 and 21 in the *Atlas for Jamaica* about settlers in the Caribbean.

Unscramble the names of each of the ethnic groups found in the English-speaking Caribbean today.

a)   n h i e c s e   _____

b)   r f c a a i n   _____

c)   e u r n p a e o   _____

d)   t e a s   d i i a n n   _____

e)   i r d a e m n n a i   _____

2 Look at the map on the next page.

a)   Add the location of the continents and countries in the box to the map.

China	Africa	South America	India	Europe

b)   Add to the map, the name of the Caribbean ethnic groups from Exercise 1, whose origin matches the countries and continents you have identified.

3 **Read the information and look at the map on page 20 in the *Atlas for Jamaica* about Amerindian civilisations. Then answer the questions.**

a) From which continent did the Tainos and Carib people (now called *Kalinagos*) who settled in the Caribbean originate?

_____

b) Name three countries in which the Tainos settled when they arrived in the Caribbean.

_____

_____

_____

c) In which Caribbean countries can we now find a large number of Carib people (Kalinagos)?

_____

_____

d) Look at the map below and complete the following:

i) Label the continents and use a small box to identify Jamaica.

ii) Name the different water bodies shown (Atlantic Ocean, Caribbean Sea and Pacific Ocean).

iii) Use arrows to show the journey of the Tainos from South America into the Caribbean.

iv) Give your map a title and insert a key and compass rose (page 4 in the *Atlas for Jamaica* provides information about the compass).

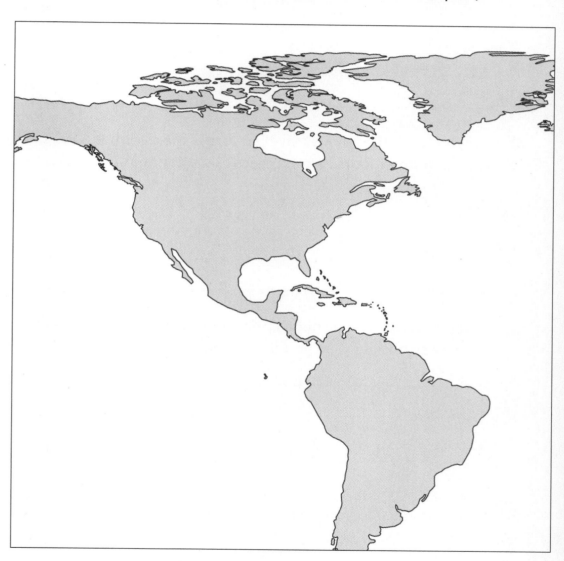

4 It is said that the Tainos came to Jamaica mainly from Venezuela in South America. Use the map on pages 12 and 13 of the *Atlas for Jamaica* to answer the questions below.

a) While in South America, do you think the Tainos faced any obstacles while making their journey? Explain.

_____

_____

_____

_____

b) Do you think the Tainos travelled across the Caribbean Sea or the Atlantic Ocean on their journey to Jamaica? Give the reason for your answer.

_____

_____

_____

_____

c) After leaving South America, the Tainos would have passed the islands of the Lesser Antilles. Can you think of why they did not settle in these islands?

_____

_____

_____

_____

d) What dangers do you think the Tainos encountered on their journey?

_____

_____

_____

_____

5 **Look at the Tainos map on page 42 in the *Atlas for Jamaica*.**

a) Use the map in the atlas to identify the location of ten Taino settlement sites in Jamaica. Use an (x) to show the location of these settlements on the map below and label each location with a number from 1 to 10. Label the parishes as well (see pages 26–27 of the *Atlas for Jamaica* for more information on parishes).

Give your map an appropriate title and insert a key to show that (x) represents 'settlement location'.

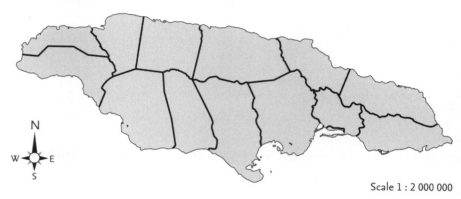

Scale 1 : 2 000 000

b) What do you notice about the location of most of the settlement sites? Why do you think this is?

_____

_____

c) Which parish has the most Tainos settlement sites?

_____

d) Name the parishes that only have one Tainos settlement site.

_____

e) To identify Tainos settlement sites, historians use rock paintings or rock carvings done by the Tainos. Name the parishes in which rock paintings have been found.

_____

6 Select three of the locations on your map in Exercise 5 and complete the table. Enter a tick (✔) in the box to answer yes and an (✗) to answer no to the questions in the columns. Use the map on pages 26–27 of the *Atlas for Jamaica* to help you.

Settlement number	Name of parish	Is the settlement close to a river?	Is the settlement close to a cave?	Is the settlement on the coast?

7 Give a reason why you think rivers, caves and the coast were important to the Tainos.

Rivers

_____

_____

Caves

_____

_____

Coast

_____

_____

8 Look at page 42 in the *Atlas for Jamaica*.

If you were a Tainos settling in Jamaica in the year 500, where would you have preferred to build your village? Give two reasons for your answer.

_____

_____

_____

9 The map below shows the site of an old Tainos settlement at White Marl in St Catherine. The settlement was built on a low hill found in the area and with a view of the sea. The Rio Cobre river is close to the site. Archeologists have found human remains, Tainos pottery and sea shells at the site.

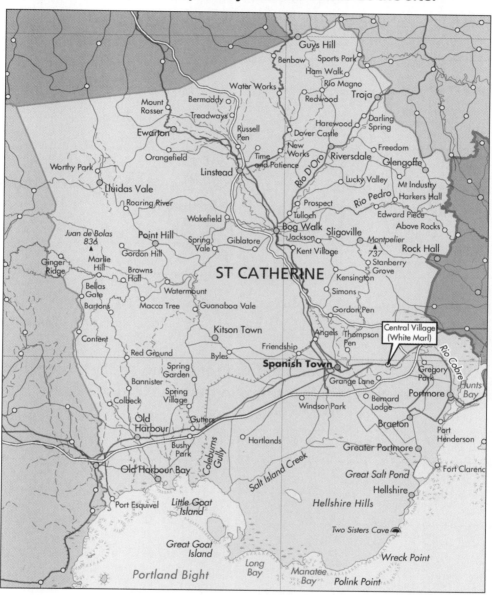

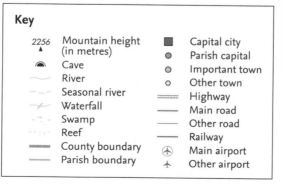

Key

2256 ▲	Mountain height (in metres)	■	Capital city
⌒	Cave	⊚	Parish capital
~~	River	⊙	Important town
–·–	Seasonal river	○	Other town
–↗–	Waterfall	====	Highway
·⸫·	Swamp	——	Main road
····	Reef	——	Other road
▬▬	County boundary	——	Railway
~~	Parish boundary	✈	Main airport
		✈	Other airport

N W E S

a) What reason or reasons do you think the Tainos had for choosing to build their settlement on a hill?

_____

_____

_____

_____

b) Using information from the map, what other advantage would the Tainos have had from settling at that location?

_____

_____

_____

_____

c) Do you think this is a good site for a community today? Using information from the map, why would you live in this area today?

_____

_____

_____

_____

Grade 4 – Term 1, Unit 2

The movement of people from one country to settle and live in another country is called *migration*. Migration is one reason for the variety of ethnic groups in Jamaica, and the other English-speaking countries in the Caribbean, that we see today. However, all of the groups did not arrive at the same time or for the same reasons. Some groups came voluntarily, while some groups were forced to come. The time in history when each group arrived and the reasons for their movement is called a *migration event*.

1 Use the *Collins Jamaican School Dictionary* to find the meaning of the words listed.

i)   heritage   _____

ii)   culture   _____

iii)   customs   _____

iv)   ethnic   _____

v)   ancestors   _____

2 Use the words from Exercise 1 to complete the text.

a)   The English speaking Caribbean is made up of many different _____ groups.

b)   Each group has a special way of doing activities such as cooking, dressing and speaking, which are all part of their _____ .

c)   The way each group does these activities is different because their _____ came from different places.

d)   Things that our parents and grandparents teach us to do, or leave for us, are part of our _____ .

e)   When the things our parents and grandparents leave for us cannot be touched, but have to be practised, they are part of what we call _____ .

3 On the map below, draw different coloured arrows showing the route taken to the Caribbean by each of the groups below.

a)   Amerindians

b)   Africans

c)   Europeans

d)   Indians

e)   Chinese

Also label on the map:

f)   the names of all the continents

g)   the Atlantic Ocean and Caribbean Sea

h)   a title and a key to show what the colours represent

4 Look at the world political and physical maps on pages 92–95 of the *Atlas for Jamaica*. Complete the crossword. (Each clue is related to the origin of ethnic groups now in the Caribbean.)

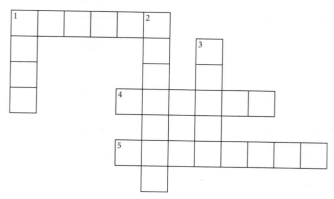

Across

1. This river flows through Brazil in South America
4. Amerinidians travelled through this country to reach South America
5. Mountains found north of India

Down

1. Mountains found in Europe
2. Abuja is the capital of this country from where some of our African ancestors came
3. Country whose capital is Beijing

5 Look at the timeline on page 42 of the *Atlas for Jamaica*. It shows major events in Jamaica's history, for example the date when the Tainos arrived and settled in Jamaica. Use the timeline to answer the following questions.

a) In what year were you born? Where on the timeline would you show this?

_____

_____

_____

b) What date did these ethnic groups arrive in Jamaica?

i) Spanish _____

ii) British _____

ii) Africans _____

6 **Create your own simple timeline by completing the diagram below.**

a) Insert on the timeline the arrival of the groups listed in 5b) on the previous page.

b) Name the events that occurred at a and b on the timeline.

c) Insert the event that took place on the date at **c** on the timeline.

d) Give the timeline a title.

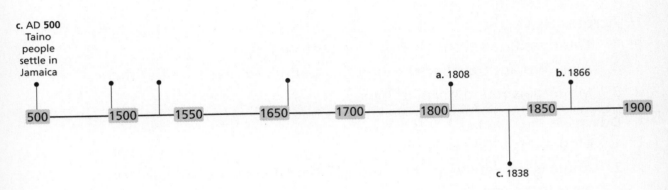

e) How long were the Spanish in Jamaica before the arrival of the British?

_____

f) Who were the first settlers in Jamaica?

_____

Grade 4 – Term 1, Unit 3

The *Order of National Hero* was established in 1969. It is the highest honour awarded by the government of Jamaica. To receive the award, a citizen of Jamaica must have done something very important for the country. Some of the Heroes even gave their lives to make Jamaica a better place. The title given to a National Hero is 'The Right Excellent'.

1 Use the *Collins Jamaican School Dictionary* to help you with the meaning of the words listed. Then match each word a) – d) with the correct definition i) – iv).

a) hero/heroine

i) A person who has done something brave or good.

b) nation

ii) Someone who is not appreciated or praised for their good work.

c) nation builder

iii) A large group of people sharing the same history and language and usually inhabiting a particular country.

d) unsung (hero)

iv) A person who has helped develop a nation gradually.

2 Read pages 42 and 43 in the *Atlas for Jamaica* and answer the questions about our National Heroes. Circle the correct answer.

a) Maroon leader during the First Maroon War.

Queen Nanny   Paul Bogle   Samuel Sharpe

b) Founded the People's Political Party.

Paul Bogle   Marcus Garvey   Usain Bolt

c) Encouraged slaves to refuse to work on Christmas Day.

Norman Manley   Queen Nanny   Samuel Sharpe

d) The first Prime Minister of Jamaica after independence.

Marcus Garvey   Sir Alexander Bustamante   Paul Bogle

e) Founded the People's National Party.

Marcus Garvey Norman Manley Marlon James

f) A Baptist deacon who paved the way for justice in the court system.

George William Gordon Paul Bogle Queen Nanny

g) Sold land cheaply to freed slaves and paid them fair wages.

Norman Manley George William Gordon Samuel Sharpe

h) Founded the Jamaica Labour Party.

George William Gordon Queen Nanny Sir Alexander Bustamante

i) Lived from 1887 to 1940.

Shelly-Ann Fraser Price Marcus Garvey Bob Marley

3 On a separate sheet of paper, create a poster about one of the National Heroes of Jamaica. Include in your poster:

a) the name of the hero/heroine

b) a picture of the hero/heroine

c) their dates of birth and death

d) a sentence on what the person did to be recognized as a national hero.

4 Read page 43 in the *Atlas for Jamaica*. Match the events with the correct date.

a) March on the Morant Bay courthouse.   i) 1929

b) Jamaica Labour Party founded.   ii) 1938

c) People's Political Party founded.   iii) 1944

d) Universal suffrage introduced to Jamaica.   iv) 1865

e) People's National Party founded.   v) 1943

Grade 4 – Term 2, Unit 1

Look at the symbol on the top left corner of page 28 of the *Atlas for Jamaica*. This symbol is called a compass rose and it shows us the directions on a map. Each lettered point is called a cardinal point. Each letter is a different direction on the map, as follows: N-north, S-south, E-east and W-west.

1 Complete the diagram of the compass by labelling all of the cardinal points.

2 Look at the map key on page 28 in the *Atlas for Jamaica*. Draw the symbol used to represent the following on the map:

a) capital city

b) cave

c) main airport

d) parish capital

e) mountain height

3 Look at the map on pages 28–29 in the *Atlas for Jamaica*. Find out what direction you would be going if you travelled:

a) from Mandeville in Manchester to Ramgoat Cave in Trelawny

b) from Montego Bay in St James to Lucea in Hanover

c) from St Ann's Bay in St Ann to May Pen in Clarendon

d) from Falmouth in Trelawny to Green Grotto Caves in St Ann

_____

e) The main airport in St James to Black River in St Elizabeth

_____

4 Look at the Jamaica East map on pages 30–31 in the *Atlas for Jamaica*. Find out what direction you would be going if you travelled:

a) from Jackson Bay Cave in Clarendon to May Pen in Clarendon

_____

b) from Morant Bay in St Thomas to Nonsuch Caves in Portland

_____

c) from the main airport near to Kingston to May Pen in Clarendon

_____

d) from Port Maria in St Mary to Two Sisters Cave in St Catherine

_____

e) from the main airport near Kingston to Morant Bay in St Thomas

_____

5 Match the clue on the left, to the parish name on the right. Use the map on pages 26–27 in the *Atlas for Jamaica* to help you.

a) St Thomas is south of this parish.   **i)** Manchester

b) A section of this parish is the most northern point   **ii)** St James
in Jamaica.

c) This parish is to the east of St James and north of Manchester. **iii)** Portland

d) Westmoreland is to the south of this parish.   **iv)** Trelawny

e) This parish has the most southern point in Jamaica.   **v)** Clarendon

f) This parish is to the east of St Elizabeth.   **vi)** Hanover

6 Look at pages 10–11 in the *Atlas for Jamaica*. Write which Caribbean capital cities can be found by travelling from Jamaica in each direction of the compass point. Use each capital city name only once.

Port of Spain	Belmopan	Port-au-Prince	Nassau
San Juan	St George's	Havana	Bridgetown
Basseterre	Roseau		

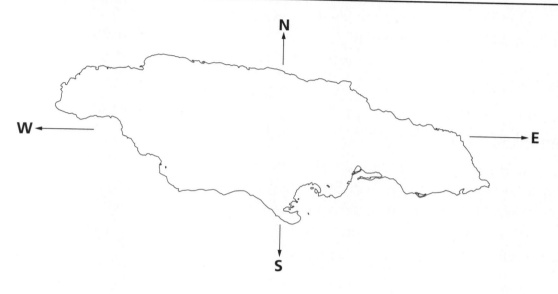

North

_____

_____

_____

South

_____

_____

_____

West

_____

_____

_____

East

_____

_____

_____

7 Use pages pages 10–11 in the *Atlas for Jamaica* to fill in the missing Caribbean countries, capital cities and cardinal directions, to complete the story below. Select your answers from the choices in brackets.

Julie is taking a cruise that involves stops at a few Caribbean capital cities. The cruise ship will leave San Juan in _____ **(Haiti, Puerto Rico)** and sail _____ **(east, west)** towards the capital city of Santo Domingo in the Dominican Republic.

From there, the ship will sail south to _____ **(Port of Spain, Port-au-Prince)** in Trinidad and Tobago.

Following the stopover in Trinidad, the ship will sail _____ **(west, north)** to arrive at St George's in Grenada and then on to _____ **(Georgetown, Bridgetown)** in Barbados where they will take part in the Crop Over Festival. This city will be the furthest _____ **(west, east)** the ship will sail.

After two days, the ship will head west to dock at _____ **(Kingstown, Kingston)** in St Vincent and the Grenadines, and then head north to dock in Roseau, _____ **(Dominica, St Lucia)**.

Julie is disappointed that the ship will not dock in _____ **(St Georges, Castries)**, St Lucia, as she really wanted to see the famous Pitons, the remains of two dormant volcanoes.

The ship will then go _____ **(south, north)** to San Juan in Puerto Rico.

For her next cruise, Julie hopes to visit _____ **(Kingstown, Kingston)** in Jamaica and travel to _____ **(Nassau, Havana)** in the Bahamas.

Grade 4 – Term 2, Unit 2

A *physical map* shows us *natural features*. Natural features are parts of the land that humans did not create. These are opposite to man-made features that humans have built. Natural features can help us pick the best place to put man-made features. For example, a road is easier to build on a flat area of land. Another name for natural features is *physical features*. Examples of physical features are our mountains and rivers.

1 Use the *Collins Jamaican School Dictionary* to help you match the words listed below with the definitions that follow.

beach	highland	lowland	cave
mountain	hill	valley	plains
plateau	river	compass	

a) A mountainous or hilly area of land.

_____

b) An instrument with a magnetic needle for finding directions.

_____

c) A large hole in rock that is underground or in the side of a cliff.

_____

d) A large flat area of land with very few trees.

_____

e) An area of sand or pebbles next to the sea.

_____

f) An area of flat, low land.

_____

g) A natural feature consisting of water flowing for a long distance between two banks.

_____

h) A rounded area of land higher than the land surrounding it.

_____

i) A very high piece of land with steep sides.

_____

j) A long stretch of land between hills, often with a river flowing through it.

_____

k) A large area of high and fairly flat land.

_____

2 Look at pages 26–27 in the *Atlas for Jamaica* and answer the following questions about Jamaica's physical features. Circle either true or false for each statement below.

a) The map shows features that are man-made.

  true   false

b) The colours on the map tell us the height of the land.

  true   false

c) The key is the part of the map that tells us what the symbols mean.

  true   false

d) The blue curvy lines on the map are the caves.

  true   false

e) There are two waterfalls shown in the parish of St Elizabeth.

  true   false

f) Nonsuch Caves can be found in the parish of Portland.

true   false

g) The highest point in St Ann is 797m at Friendship.

true   false

h) Most of the inland area is lowland (0–100m).

true   false

i) The length of the coastline is 1022 km.

true   false

3 The rivers and plains of Jamaica are two of the island's most important physical features. Rivers are found in most of the parishes, but plains can be found in fewer parishes. Use the map on pages 26–27 in the *Atlas for Jamaica* to complete the table below.

Parish	Name of plains	Name of river(s)
Hanover		
Westmoreland		
St James		
St Elizabeth		
Trelawny		
Manchester		
St Ann		
Clarendon		
St Catherine		
St Mary		
St Andrew		
Portland		
St Thomas		

4 **Use the map on pages 26–27 in the *Atlas for Jamaica* to help you label the map below.**

a) Draw in and label the following rivers: Plantain Garden River, Buff Bay River, Black River, Rio Cobre, Morant River.

b) Shade and label the following plains: Georges Plain and Pedro Plains.

c) Add a title to your map, a compass rose and a key.

Remember to use appropriate colours for your rivers and plains. Remember also that a good map is easy to read, so use sharp coloured pencils to make your lines, labels and shading clean and clear.

5 **Look at the map on pages 26–27 in the *Atlas for Jamaica* and answer the questions.**

a) Name the river in Westmorland parish that flows west into Long Bay.

_____

b) The Wag Water River flows through which two parishes?

_____

c) Name the river that separates the parishes of St Ann and St Mary.

_____

d) Underline the two words that best describe the plains of Jamaica.
inland   coastal   southern   northern

6 Look at the physical map on pages 26–27, the agriculture map on page 37 and the industry map on page 38 in the *Atlas for Jamaica*. Answer the questions below.

G4

a) What type of crops are grown on Georges Plain in Westmoreland?

_____

b) Name three industries found along the Rio Minho in Clarendon.

_____

c) What industry do Georges Plain and Pedro Plain have in common?

_____

d) Name the river found close to where coffee is grown in St Thomas.

_____

7 From Exercise 6, we can see that our plains and rivers are important for farming and industrial activities.

a) Give one reason why you think plains are good for the planting of crops, especially on a large scale.

_____

_____

_____

b) In what ways do you think farmers use the rivers close to them?

_____

_____

_____

c) Sometimes our rivers are affected negatively by what we do. How do you think farming and industrial activities can impact our rivers?

_____

_____

_____

d) Along with farming and industry, what else do you think our rivers and plains are used for?

_____

_____

_____

Grade 4 – Term 2, Unit 3

A *political map* shows us how humans have divided up the land to make it easier to manage. The lines on a political map are called *boundaries*. An area surrounded by a set of boundaries is called a *political division*. Political divisions can have many names such as states, counties and parishes. Political maps can change because boundary lines are imaginary and can be moved when better ways to divide the land are found. Political maps also show capital cities and major towns in a country.

1 What is the name of the parish in which you live? Do you know how large this parish is?

_____

_____

2 Look at pages 32–33 in the *Atlas for Jamaica*. Use information on these pages to create a ranking list organizing the parishes of Jamaica from largest to smallest.

	Parish	Area
1		
2		
3		
4		
5		
6		
7		
8		
9		
10		
11		
12		
13		
14		

3 Look at pages 32–33 in the *Atlas for Jamaica* and the information on the 2016 population in each parish. Create a ranking list organizing the parishes in each county from most populated to least populated.

Cornwall

	Parish	Population
1		
2		
3		
4		
5		

Middlesex

	Parish	Population
1		
2		
3		
4		
5		

Surrey

	Parish	Population
1		
2		
3		
4		

4 Each parish in Jamaica has a capital city. Look at pages 28–33 in the *Atlas for Jamaica* to complete the table. For each parish, state whether the capital is inland or coastal.

Parish	Parish capital	Inland/Coastal

5 Look at the table you have completed in Exercise 4 and answer the questions.

a) Are most of the parish capitals inland or coastal?

_____

_____

_____

_____

b) What do you think are two advantages of a coastal parish capital?

_____

_____

_____

_____

c) What do you think are two advantages of an inland parish capital?

_____

_____

_____

_____

6 Complete the map below. Remember that the key must show what each colour and symbol used represents.

a) Label each parish and county.

b) Insert and label each parish capital in their correct location. Use different symbols for inland and coastal parish capitals.

c) Shade each county using a different coloured pencil.

d) Add a compass rose and a key to your map.

e) Give your map an appropriate title.

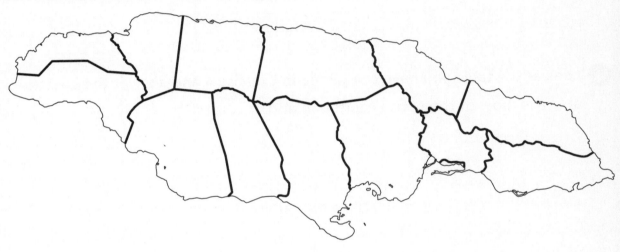

7 **Did you know that the name, size and number of parishes have changed many times? Jamaica did not always have 14 parishes.**

Compare the maps at the bottom of page 32 in the *Atlas for Jamaica* with the parish map in the middle of pages 32–33 to see some of the changes made to the parishes. Circle the correct answer from each set of choices.

a) How many of the parishes from 1664 still exist today?

    3   5   14

b) Which eastern parish was present in 1738 but not in 1664?

    Portland   St James   St Elizabeth

c) How many parishes were added to the map by 1738?

    11   12   18

d) Which parish was created when Westmoreland was divided?

    St James   Hanover   St Mary

e) Trelawny used to be a part of which parish?

    St Ann   St James   St Thomas in the East

f) Which parish became a part of modern day St Catherine?

    St Thomas in the Vale   St David   Port Royal

g) St George and St Marie were joined to create which parish?

    Manchester   St Andrew   St Mary

h) Parts of Manchester and Clarendon used to make up this parish.

    St John   Port Royal   Vere

i) In 1738, this parish was created by dividing St Andrew.

    Kingston   Westmoreland   St Catherine

j) Between 1664 and 1738 the number of inland parishes increased by:

    1   2   4

8 If you had the power to change the parishes, what kind of changes would you make? Draw new parish boundaries on the map of Jamaica and label the parish names. Give two reasons for the changes you would make.

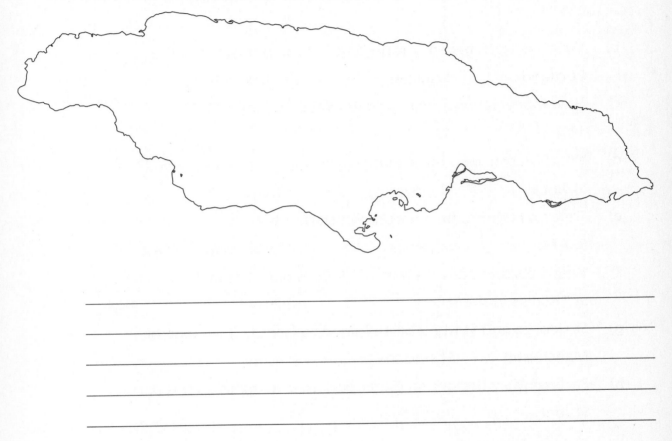

_____

_____

_____

_____

_____

Grade 4 – Term 3, Unit 1

The weather tells us what is happening in the atmosphere in a given time and place. The weather is important because it is easier to do some things in certain weather. For example it is much nicer to go on a picnic when it is a warm, sunny day. Some weather can even be dangerous and special actions must be taken to stay safe. A person who studies the weather is called a *meteorologist*.

1 Read page 35 in the *Atlas for Jamaica*. Find the 15 weather words hidden in the word search puzzle. They may be found vertical, horizontal, diagonal or backwards.

air pressure	barometer	cloud cover	humidity
hurricane	meteorologist	rain gauge	rainfall
storm	sunshine	temperature	thermometer
tropical	wind speed	wind vane	

M	G	R	G	R	W	R	H	F	R	B	T	R	T	Q
W	E	S	E	F	A	U	E	E	U	H	M	A	K	K
L	A	T	J	V	M	I	T	B	E	S	E	I	T	Q
I	A	E	E	I	O	E	N	R	N	N	O	N	E	M
F	I	C	D	O	M	C	M	G	A	W	T	F	M	D
C	S	I	I	O	R	O	D	V	U	A	T	A	P	E
Y	T	W	R	P	M	O	D	U	Q	A	T	L	E	E
Y	S	A	L	E	O	N	L	H	O	A	G	L	R	P
K	B	G	T	S	I	R	M	O	Z	L	Q	E	A	S
D	N	E	H	W	Z	Y	T	Z	G	L	C	D	T	D
P	R	E	N	I	H	S	N	U	S	I	O	D	U	N
E	R	U	S	S	E	R	P	R	I	A	S	T	R	I
H	U	R	R	I	C	A	N	E	T	L	V	T	E	W
E	Q	Z	C	Y	Q	X	Q	T	S	T	O	R	M	K
O	C	A	R	Q	N	K	Z	S	Q	C	A	Q	W	N

2 Information about the weather can also be shown on maps and in diagrams. Read carefully the information on page 34 in the *Atlas for Jamaica* about wind, rainfall and temperature in Jamaica. Complete each sentence by filling in the blank space.

a)   The wind in Port Antonio normally blows from the _____ direction.

b)   The parish that receives the most rainfall is _____.

c)   Look at the rainfall graphs for the different towns. These show that the rainiest month in most parts of Jamaica is _____.

d)   Look at the temperature graphs. The area with the coolest temperatures all year is _____.

e)   On the seasonal rainfall map for March, it is showing that the driest areas in the south are in the parishes of _____ and _____. These areas get less than _____ of rainfall in this month.

f)   The rainfall graph for Montego Bay shows that average rainfall in March is about 50 mm and in September, about 150 mm. This means average rainfall in Montego Bay from March to September increases by _____ mm.

g)   Kingston receives less than 50 mm of rainfall for _____ months of the year.

h)   The temperature in Runaway Bay is higher than 25°C for _____ months of the year.

i)   The maximum temperature recorded for Negril is _____, while the minimum temperature is _____.

3 Write a journal entry of about 100 words describing some of the things you would do to prepare for the hurricane season. Use an extra sheet of paper if you need to.

_____

_____

_____

_____

_____

4 Read the section on hurricanes on page 35 in the *Atlas for Jamaica*. Match
the beginnings of the sentences a) – i) to the correct ending i) – ix).

Beginnings

a)   A total of 45 people were killed in Jamaica

b)   A hurricane may get stronger after making landfall,

c)   After 1979, the government wanted to help Jamaicans deal with natural
disasters and

d)   A storm surge is a sudden, powerful wave that

e)   In 2008, the tropical storm Gustav destroyed 70–85% of

f)   Due to its location in the Atlantic hurricane belt, Jamaica is

g)   Jamaica is vulnerable to severe flooding and landslides, which sometimes

h)   In 2007, Hurricane Dean

i)   Pictures of the Earth from space can help us see

Endings

i)   destroyed 2854 houses in Jamaica.

ii)   established the Office of Disaster Preparedness and Emergency Management.

iii)   sweeps inland from the sea.

iv)   where a hurricane is and the path it takes.

v)   by Hurricane Gilbert in 1988.

vi)   causing even more damage.

vii)   cause more damage than the winds and storm surge.

viii)   regularly hit by hurricanes and tropical storms.

ix)   the banana crop in Jamaica.

Grade 4 – Term 3, Unit 2

The *solar system* is made up of *planets* moving around the Sun in space. This movement is called a revolution or an *orbit*. Each planet in the solar system has special characteristics; however, only planet *Earth* is home to life.

There are other objects in our solar system such as *moons* and *comets*. Learning about the solar system is important if we want to find out how we may be able to live on other planets someday. People who study the solar system are called *astronomers*.

1 Read pages 8–9 in the *Atlas for Jamaica* and unscramble the words about the solar system. Then, complete the sentences.

a)   r t b o i   _____

b)   a p l e t n s   _____

c)   c u e r m y r   _____

d)   a o s l r   m s e y s t   _____

e)   v i g r a y t   _____

i)   There are eight _____ that go round the Sun.

ii)   _____ is the closet planet to the Sun.

iii)   The Sun uses its pull of _____ to keep objects in its _____.

iv)   The _____ _____ is the Sun, planets, and the many objects that orbit it.

2 Read pages 8–9 in the *Atlas for Jamaica* to complete the following questions.

a)   The asteroid belt is found between Jupiter and which other planet?

_____

b)   What planet is the largest in the solar system?

_____

c)   How many dwarf planets are there in our solar system?

_____

d)   How long is the length of a year on Uranus?

_____

e)   How far is Venus from the Sun?

_____

f)   What is the distance between Earth and Mars?

_____

g)   Which planet has the shortest day?

_____

h)   Which planet is fifth in line from the Sun?

_____

i)   Name two other objects besides planets and moons that can be found orbiting the Sun.

_____

3   Read pages 8–9 in the *Atlas for Jamaica* and complete the table.

	Distance from the Sun (million km)	Length of year	Length of day
Mercury			
Venus			
Earth			
Mars			
Jupiter			
Saturn			
Uranus			
Neptune			

4   Look at the table you have completed in Exercise 3 and answer the questions.

a)   Which planet has the longest year?

_____

b)   Which planet is 1427 million km from the Sun?

_____

c)   Which planet has a year that lasts 365 days and 6 hours?

_____

d)   Which planet has a day that lasts 59 of our Earth days?

_____

e)   Which planet has its length of day as 24 hours and 37 minutes?

_____

f)   On which planet would you have to wait 165 Earth years before you could celebrate your birthday?

_____

5 Use pages 8 and 9 of the *Atlas for Jamaica* and coloured pencils to draw your own simple diagram of the solar system in the box. Draw the planets in the correct positions from the Sun and be sure to label each planet correctly.

G4

Grade 4 – Term 3, Unit 3

Jamaica is considered a *tropical island*. It has good rainfall and heat, therefore many plants are able to grow well on the island. However, all the plants in Jamaica are not the same. Some have always been in Jamaica, even before humans. Some were brought by humans accidentally and some were introduced to grow for food. All the plants together in an area are called *vegetation* and a *land cover map* is a good way to find out the types of plants that grow in a country. A person who studies plants is called a *botanist*.

1 Use the *Collins Jamaican School Dictionary* to find the meaning of the words listed.

a) forest

_____

b) habitat

_____

c) deforestation

_____

d) interdependent

_____

e) nature

_____

2 Use the physical map of Jamaica on pages 26–27 and the land cover map on page 36 of the *Atlas for Jamaica* to learn more about vegetation types in Jamaica and where they are found. Match the clues a–d to the correct answers i–iv.

a)   The highland physical feature in the east covered with evergreen forest.

b)   The most southern area of wetland is found here.

c)   The largest urban area is found in this parish.

d)   The second largest area of evergreen forest is found in this part of the island.

i)   Blue Mountains

ii)   The Cockpit Country

iii)   West Harbour, Clarendon

iv)   St Andrew

3 Read pages 22, 23 and 36 in the *Atlas for Jamaica* to complete the sentences by using each word from the box.

endangered	pollution	deforestation
acidification	climate change	bleaching
wind	vegetation	

a)   _____ is the cutting down of areas of forest.

b)   _____ has led to the warming of the sea and also to its
_____.

c)   Jamaica has a total of 28 _____ species, including 7 birds, 8 reptiles and 5 mammals.

d)   Coral _____ is the effect of disease causing coral to die.

e)   _____ power can help to reduce energy costs and dependence on oil.

f)   Water _____ is a major environmental problem, especially in coastal areas polluted by industrial waste, sewage and oil spills.

g)   Threats to the environment in Jamaica include air pollution, coral bleaching and the loss of areas of _____ for houses, factories and roads.

4 Examine the images below showing deforestation and read page 100 in the *Atlas for Jamaica* about deforestation.

a) Based on these images, what impact do you think deforestation may end up causing? State three problems.

_____

_____

_____

_____

_____

b) What would you suggest to help reduce the problems caused by deforestation? Make two suggestions.

_____

_____

_____

_____

_____

5 Using the pie chart and bar graph on page 36 of the *Atlas for Jamaica*, answer the following questions.

a) What was the total percentage of protected forested areas in Jamaica in 2014?

_____

b) Which is larger, the total area of forests in Jamaica or areas of other land?

_____

c) Did the total area of protected forest increase between 2009 and 2014?

_____

d) For what reason(s) do you think some forest areas are protected by law?

_____

_____

_____

Grade 4 – Term 3, Unit 4

Some human activities can be harmful to the *environment*. It is important that anything we do respects the environment and does not cause any lasting damage. It is our responsibility to take care of the environment, because important *resources* like water, air and soil come from the natural world.

1 Use your *Collins Jamaican School Dictionary* to write the definition of each of the following words.

a) pollution

_____

b) waste

_____

c) damage

_____

d) recycle

_____

e) reduce

_____

2 Use pages 22, 23 and 36 of the *Atlas for Jamaica* to complete the questions below.

a) What effect has coral reef damage had in the Caribbean?

_____

b) What human activity creates red mud lakes?

_____

c) The cane toad, lionfish and casuarina trees are all types of what type of species?

_____

d) Name an endangered species of whale.

_____

e) Using wind power can help Caribbean countries use less of which fuel?

_____

f) Which country in the Caribbean produces the highest amount of carbon dioxide per person?

_____

g) What percentage of forest cover did Jamaica lose between 1990 and 2010?

_____

h) What type of pollution is created by mining bauxite?

_____

i) Water pollution is a major problem in which two urban areas of Jamaica?

_____

j) Why is the Jamaican iguana critically endangered?

_____

3 **Examine the image below, then respond to the questions that follow.**

a) What type of pollution do you see in the image?

_____

_____

b) Suggest three things that may have contributed to this type of pollution.

_____

_____

_____

_____

_____

c) What kind of problems do you think may develop from this type of pollution?

_____

_____

_____

_____

d) If you were the mayor of Montego Bay, what would you do to stop this problem? Suggest two things.

_____

_____

_____

_____

Grade 5 – Term 1, Unit 1

Colonisation happened when European explorers tried to find new *trade routes* to the east to find spices, which were very valuable. Some explorers, such as Christopher Columbus, thought they could find these new routes by sailing west, where they came across lands they did not expect and new people they had never met before.

These new lands became colonies, as the Europeans later settled and claimed these places as their own. Many other Europeans came after but for other reasons. While some came to find wealth, others came to find land and escape strife in their homeland. These new lands were very good for farming crops and so some Europeans established large farms called plantations. To provide *labour* for these plantations, many Africans were forced into *slavery* and transported from West Africa to countries in the Caribbean.

The plantation system was very cruel as the enslaved Africans had no rights and worked for long hours with no pay. They were considered the property of the plantation owners, who could sell them if they wished. The enslaved Africans often *resisted* and *rebelled* to free themselves and be treated like humans instead of property.

1 Use the *Collins Jamaican School Dictionary* to find the meaning of the words listed.

a) ancestor

_____

b) colonize

_____

c) plantation

_____

d) slave

_____

e) emancipation

_____

f) abolition

_____

2 **Read pages 20–21 and 42–43 in the** *Atlas for Jamaica* **and complete the paragraphs below using the words in the box provided.**

Africans	slaves	explorers
plantations	colonies	slave labour
migrated	multicultural	Atlantic Ocean

a) European _____ arrived in the Caribbean in their search for new trade routes to the east. They sailed from Europe across the _____ where they found new lands. They later settled these lands setting up _____ where more Europeans could come to settle

b) At the beginning of the 16th century _____ were captured and transported across the Atlantic in ships to work as _____ in the Caribbean. Many died on the three-month voyage.

c) This forced migration of people from West Africa to the Caribbean involved taking goods from Europe to West Africa in exchange for persons who would be used as _____.

d) The enslaved Africans were forced to work on _____ which grew crops like sugar cane. Jamaica became one of the world's main producers and exporters of sugar using a plantation system and slave labour.

e) Some peoples _____ to the Caribbean of their own free will from Africa, Europe and Asia – the greatest numbers coming from India, Indonesia and China.

f) The Caribbean is now a _____ area as different groups have brought their own languages, religions and cultures to the region and integrated with existing communities.

3 Read pages 20–21 in the *Atlas for Jamaica* and complete the names of ethnic groups that came to the Caribbean.

a) _ n d i _ n

b) M i _ _ l e   E a s _ _ r n

c) A _ r _ c _ n

d) A m _ r i n _ i a _

e) _ u r o _ e a n

f) C _ i n _ _ e

4 Do you remember learning about timelines in your previous grade? Timelines are used to show important dates and events. You will make your own timeline to show important events related to the Europeans and Africans. Use page 42 of the *Atlas for Jamaica* to insert the following events and their dates correctly on the timeline, and give your timeline an appropriate title.

To do this, you will first need to draw a 10 cm horizontal line below, and then divide your line into equal intervals of 2 cm. Each interval will represent 100 years, so start your timeline at 1400.

a) The arrival of Christopher Columbus from Spain.

b) The capture of Jamaica by the British from the Spanish.

c) The arrival of the first group of Africans.

d) The abolition of the slave trade.

e) The emancipation of the Africans from slavery.

5 **Complete the following using the timeline you created.**

a) Calculate the number years between the arrival of the first group of Africans and the emancipation of the Africans from slavery.

_____

b) Before the enslaved Africans were emancipated, a law was passed to first end the trading of slaves. How long after the abolition of the slave trade did emancipation take place?

_____

6 **The Europeans who came to Jamaica were mainly from Spain and Britain (now the United Kingdom). Use page 86 of the _Atlas for Jamaica_ to label these countries on the map below.**

7 **The Africans who came to Jamaica, and other parts of the Caribbean, came mainly from a region called West Africa. Some of the countries included Nigeria, Ghana, Sierra Leone, Senegal, Togo and Cameroon.**

Look at page 82 in the *Atlas for Jamaica* and label these countries on the map below. Insert the capital city for each country (see page 84) and complete the map by adding a title and key.

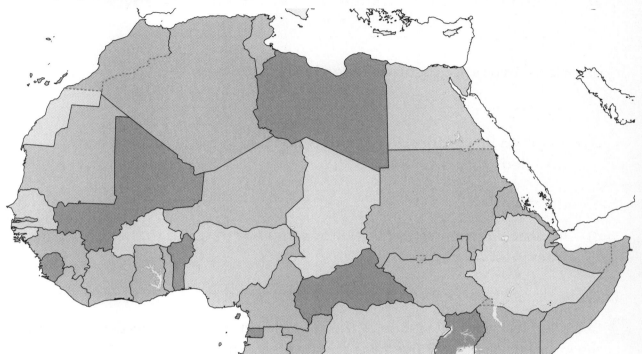

8 Look at the political map of Africa on page 82 and the political map of the world (pages 92–93) in the *Atlas for Jamaica* to complete the questions below.

a) Which of the countries identified in Exercise 7 is the largest?

_____

b) Name two other countries found in West Africa.

_____

c) To get to West Africa, in what direction would the Europeans have travelled?

_____

d) In what direction would the Europeans have travelled to the Caribbean from West Africa?

_____

9 Extended learning: select one of the countries identified in Exercise 7 and use the internet to research five facts about this country.

_____

_____

_____

_____

_____

Grade 5 – Term 1, Unit 2

Fighting for *freedom* was very difficult. This is because the *planters* had the most money and power and also set the laws of the country. Therefore, it was *heroic* to do anything that the planters did not like. Heroes like Queen Nanny and Samuel Sharpe fought against the system of slavery, while Paul Bogle and George William Gordon fought for better conditions and *equal rights* for the people after slavery ended. Many persons lived in poverty and had no jobs or land even though they were now free. These heroes tried to make Jamaica a better country.

1 Use the *Collins Jamaican School Dictionary* to complete the following questions.

a) What is a protest?

_____

_____

b) Define social injustice.

_____

_____

c) Write a synonym for the adjective 'just'.

_____

_____

d) Define the word 'execute'.

_____

_____

e) Write two synonyms for the word 'rebellion'.

_____

_____

2 'Nanny of the Maroons' is our only female National Hero. She lived during a period when slavery existed in Jamaica and when the British controlled Jamaica. Use the internet to do some research, and read pages 42–43 in the *Atlas for Jamaica*, to answer the following questions.

a) Who were the 'Maroons'?

_____

_____

b) How did Maroon communities begin?

_____

_____

c) Nanny is described as a great 'military strategist'. What do you think this means?

_____

_____

d) When did the First Maroon War occur?

_____

_____

e) How did the Maroons cause problems for the British?

_____

_____

f) From your research, why do you think Queen Nanny became a hero?

_____

_____

3 Add to the map below, the following:

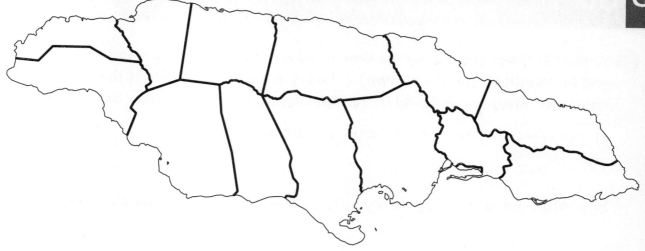

a)   The Maroon areas and towns on page 42 in the *Atlas for Jamaica*.

b)   Use pages 26–27 of the *Atlas for Jamaica* to label the two main mountain ranges where the Maroon settlements were found.

c)   Use the land cover map on page 36 of the *Atlas for Jamaica* to identify the type of land cover where the Maroon settlements were found.

d)   Label the modern day parishes, add a key and compass.

4 Using the land cover map on page 36 of the *Atlas for Jamaica*, think about the following questions.

a)   What advantage do you think the Maroons had as a result of living in these areas?

_____

_____

_____

b)   What challenges do you think they faced by settling in these areas?

_____

_____

_____

5 Samuel Sharpe lived during the time of slavery in Jamaica. He was a slave himself and he fought to end the system of slavery. He was the leader of the 'Christmas Rebellion'. Read pages 42–43 in the *Atlas for Jamaica* and answer the questions.

a) In what year was the 'Christmas Rebellion'?

_____

b) What did Samuel Sharpe encourage the other enslaved people to do?

_____

c) Do you think this was a good approach to get what they wanted? Explain.

_____

_____

d) How soon after the rebellion were the enslaved Africans emancipated?

_____

e) Do you think the rebellion influenced the emancipation of the enslaved Africans? Explain.

_____

_____

6 Paul Bogle and George William Gordon worked to help improve the lives of people during the period after slavery ended. Read pages 42–43 in the *Atlas for Jamaica* and answer the questions.

a) What was Paul Bogle's profession?

_____

b) In what year did the Morant Bay Rebellion take place?

_____

c) How many years after slavery ended did the Morant Bay Rebellion take place?

_____

d) What was Bogle fighting against?

_____

e) Explain why poverty would have made it difficult for people to get just treatment in courts.

_____

_____

f) George William Gordon sold land cheaply to the free, formerly enslaved people. Explain why this would be considered a heroic thing to do.

_____

_____

7 **Read page 43 in the _Atlas for Jamaica_ and answer the questions about modern-day famous Jamaicans.**

a) Who is the fastest sprinter of all time in the 100 m and 200 m?

_____

b) With which sport would you associate Michael Holding, Courtney Walsh and Chris Gayle?

_____

c) In which area of the arts were the following people famous:

i) Bob Marley _____

ii) Barrington 'Barry' Watson _____

iii) Marlon James _____

iv) Louise Bennett-Coverley _____

v) Lee 'Scratch' Perry _____

Grade 5 – Term 1, Unit 3

The Caribbean is a *culturally diverse* place. This means that many different cultures from many parts of the world come together. Sometimes diversity may cause strife and problems, but the Caribbean is still one of the most *peaceful* places to live! Learning about other islands' *culture* and what makes them *unique* helps us to *appreciate* the *similarities* and *respect* the *differences*.

1 Use the *Collins Jamaican School Dictionary* to look up the words below, and then unscramble each set of words connected with the given term.

a) **culture**

t r a s _____

d s i e a _____

o c u t s s m _____

b) **heritage**

s s n s p o e s s o i _____

d r t i a o t n i s _____

n e a g e t i o n r _____

c) **diverse/diversify**

f d i e f t r e n _____

a v i r e t y _____

d) **cultural heritage**

l i t e e r a u r t _____

i s t u a r l _____

2 **The language of the Caribbean is quite diverse because of the different groups that settled in the region.**

Look at pages 18–19 in the *Atlas for Jamaica* to identify the language of the different Caribbean states on the map below. Colour each territory as shown in the key.

English speaking territories – yellow

Spanish speaking territories – blue

French speaking territories – green

Dutch speaking territories – red

3 **Some Caribbean states have an unofficial language called a Creole. In Jamaica, our Creole language is called Patois (Patwa). Use pages 46–72 in the *Atlas for Jamaica* to complete the table below. Use:**

- a C for countries that have a Creole language
- an S for countries that have Spanish as a language
- an F for countries that have French as a language
- a triangle for those countries that speak any other language

Anguilla		Dominica		St-Barthélemy	
Antigua and Barbuda		Dominican Republic		St Eustatius	
Aruba		Grenada		St Kitts and Nevis	
The Bahamas		Guadeloupe		St Lucia	
Barbados		Guyana		St-Martin	
Belize		Haiti		Sint Maarten	
Bonaire		Martinique		St Vincent and the Grenadines	
British Virgin Islands		Montserrat		Trinidad and Tobago	
Cayman Islands		Puerto Rico		Turks and Caicos Islands	
Cuba		Saba		US Virgin Islands	
Curaçao					

4 **Another aspect of Caribbean culture is the different festivals and celebrations each country has. Use the internet and pages 46–72 of the *Atlas for Jamaica* to research the festivals below and complete the table.**

Festival/Celebration	Country/countries	Date celebrated	Reason for celebrating
Mashramani			
Carnival			
Crop Over			
Vincy Mas			
Jonkanoo			
Grand Gala			

5 **Look at the table you created in Exercise 3.**

a) Select ONE Spanish speaking country and ONE French speaking country and use the internet to research about these elements of culture of those countries: food, religion, music, dance, dress. Present the information in the table below.

Country	Food	Religion	Music/dance	Dress

b) Compare these countries with Jamaica to identify similarities and differences in the culture.

_____

_____

_____

6 **Interview members of your family to find out answers to the questions below.**

a) What are some of the things that threaten culture in the Caribbean?

_____

_____

_____

b) How can we protect and preserve our culture?

_____

_____

_____

7 Let us extend our knowledge of our Caribbean neighbours. Use pages 46–72 in the *Atlas for Jamaica* to answer the questions below.

a) Name the prehistoric inhabitants of the Bahamas.

_____

b) What is the capital of the Turks and Caicos Islands?

_____

c) The Cuban revolution occurred in this year.

_____

d) This reptile is only found on Grand Cayman.

_____

e) What event made Haiti the first independent country in the Caribbean?

_____

f) The Dominican Republic has independence on which two days of the year?

_____

g) What happened on Transfer Day in the U.S. Virgin Islands?

_____

h) Name the national flower of St Kitts and Nevis.

_____

i) Name the national bird of Montserrat.

_____

j) What is in the dish called Matete in Guadelope?

_____

k) Name the national flower of Dominica.

_____

l) Name the St Lucian who has won the Nobel Prize for Literature.

_____

m) What spice is Grenada most known for producing?

_____

n) What event is held in Trinidad and Tobago on the Monday and Tuesday before Ash Wednesday?

_____

o) On what date does Guyana celebrate Republic Day?

_____

G5 — Why does erosion occur and how does it affect the land?

Soil is created by **weathering** processes. These are processes that break down rock from large blocks into fine grains. Weathering releases nutrients from rocks and allows water to soak into the Earth's surface, creating a good environment for plants to grow and burrowing animals to live. Movement of water and wind over the soil transports it away – this is called **soil erosion** and is a natural process. However, human activities can cause too much water or wind to move over the soil, or can make soil grains too loose. This causes **accelerated soil erosion**, when soil is removed faster than it can be created.

1 Use the *Collins Jamaican School Dictionary* to find the meaning of each of the following words.

a) erode

_____

b) erosion

_____

c) topsoil

_____

d) deposition

_____

e) sediment

_____

2 Use the maps and information on pages 100–101 of the *Atlas for Jamaica* and the *Collins Jamaican School Dictionary* to answer the following questions:

a) What is deforestation?

_____

_____

b) What are two human activities that can cause deforestation?

_____

_____

c) In what way can deforestation be caused accidentally?

_____

_____

d) What is desertification?

_____

_____

e) Define the following terms:

   i) fertile land

_____

_____

   ii) arid land

_____

_____

3 Organize the following statements to explain how deforestation can cause soil erosion and desertification. Write numbers from 1 to 8 on the lines to show the correct order.

a) Humans clear forests to make space for cows to graze. _____

b) Without grass and small plants to absorb rain, rainwater cannot soak into the land. _____

c) The river water rises since it cannot flow and the river floods its banks. _____

d) Soil without nutrients is infertile and even small plants and grass can no longer grow. _____

e) Flooded rivers lift and wash away even more topsoil and wash even more nutrients from the soil. _____

f) Since tree roots are not present to slow down the water flow, rain flows quickly over the land and washes soil into rivers. _____

g) The land therefore becomes dry and empty, like a desert. _____

h) Rivers become choked with soil, blocking the water from flowing into the sea. _____

4 Page 36 of the *Atlas for Jamaica* shows an image of mining activities in Jamaica.

a) How can this activity lead to soil erosion?

_____

_____

b) State how soil erosion can be harmful to:

i) crop farming

_____

_____

ii)   livestock farming

_____

_____

iii) water supply

_____

_____

iv)   wildlife

_____

_____

5 **The two maps on pages 100–101 of the *Atlas for Jamaica* give us information on deforestation across the globe.**

a)   From which of the two maps are we able to get more information about deforestation across the globe?

_____

_____

b)   Write a brief summary explaining why your selection is accurate. Use evidence from the map to support your answer.

_____

_____

_____

_____

_____

_____

_____

_____

_____

Grade 5 – Term 2, Unit 2

You may remember, in Grade 4, term 2, unit 1, that each lettered point on a compass is called a cardinal point. These are: north, south, east and west.

We can divide the compass further into four more directions, midway between each of the cardinal points.

These are called the inter-cardinal points – northeast, southeast, northwest and southwest.

1 Complete the diagram of the compass below by labelling all of the cardinal points and inter-cardinal points.

2 Use pages 26–27 in the *Atlas for Jamaica* to find out what direction you would be travelling in for the following:

a) From Smokey Hole Cave to Rose Hill in Manchester.

_____

b) Along the Morant River in St Thomas to Morant Bay.

_____

c) From Orange Hill in Westmoreland to South Negril Point.

_____

d) From Good Hope Mountain to Catherine's Peak in St Andrew.

_____

e) From Cockpit to Ramgoat Cave in Trelawny.

_____

f) Along the Plantain Garden River to Holland Bay in St Thomas.

_____

g) From Great Goat Island close to St Catherine to Dolphin Island close to Clarendon.

_____

h) From Albion in St Ann to Juan de Bolas in St Catherine.

_____

i) From Green Grotto Caves in St Ann to Windsor Cave in Trelawny.

_____

j) From Y.S. Falls to Maggotty Falls in St Elizabeth.

_____

3 Use pages 28–31 of the *Atlas for Jamaica* to complete the crossword.
A page tip has been given for each clue.

Across

1. The first important town travelling west from Balaclava, St Elizabeth parish. [page 29]

5. This coastal landform is to the east of Port Royal, Kingston parish. [page 30]

8. The parish capital east of Montego Bay. [page 29]

9. The first important town travelling north from Cave Valley, St Ann. [page 29]

10. You must pass this important town travelling northwest from Seaforth to Cedar Valley, St Thomas parish. [page 31]

11. To travel northeast from Gayle to Oracabessa, St Mary parish, you must cross this river. [page 30]

13. The second important town travelling southeast from Lluidas Vale, St Catherine. [page 30]

14. The town you would arrive at if you cross The Cockpit Country travelling west from Spring Garden, Trelawny parish. [page 28]

Down

2. The area of water you would sail through travelling south, from North Negril Point to South Negril Point. [page 28]

3. The first town on the southeastern road from Royal Flat in Manchester parish. [page 29]

4. The important town in the southwesterly direction from Lucea, Hanover parish. [page 28]

6. The important town found to the northeast of Harbour View, St Andrew parish. [page 31]

7. The highland area you would pass through heading northwest from Manchioneal to Windsor, Portland parish. [page 31]

9. The second town travelling northeast from Savanna-la-Mar. [page 28]

12. The last other town on the southern road between Maypen and Lionel Town, Clarendon parish. [page 30]

4 Use pages 28–31 of the *Atlas for Jamaica* to find out what direction you would be travelling in for the following:

Jamaica West (pages 28–29)

a) From Mandeville in Manchester to May Pen in Clarendon.

_____

b) From Savanna-la-mar in Westmoreland to Montego Bay in St James.

_____

c) From Discovery Bay in St Ann to Albert Town in Trelawny.

_____

d) From Lucea in Hanover to Black River in St Elizabeth.

_____

e) From Cross Keys in Manchester to Mandeville.

_____

Jamaica East (pages 30–31)

a) From Kingston to Bog Walk in St Catherine.

_____

b) From Port Antonio in Portland to Port Maria in St Mary.

_____

c) From Yallahs Point in St Thomas to Port Antonio in Portland.

_____

d) From St Ann's Bay in St Ann to Spanish Town in St Catherine.

_____

e) From Spanish Town in St Catherine to Half Way Tree in St Andrew.

_____

5 **Use pages 10–11 of the _Atlas for Jamaica_ to circle the correct answer from each set of choices.**

a) What direction would you travel to arrive at Havana from Kingston?

south   northwest   northeast

b) Santiago is in what direction from Santo Domingo?

north   northwest   east

c) Which island is south of Sint Maarten?

Anguilla   Puerto Rico   Saba

d) What is the most southern French territory?

Martinique   Guadeloupe   St Lucia

e) What direction would you travel to arrive at Castries from Kingstown?

south   southeast   north

f) What direction would you travel to arrive at St Georges from Bridgetown?

north   southeast   southwest

g) What direction is Fort-de-France (Martinique) from Mayagüez (Puerto Rico)?

southeast   west   north

h) What direction would you travel to arrive at Willemstad (Curaçao) from Kralendijk (Bonaire)?

south   west   north

i) Which city is to the south of St George's, Grenada?

Caracas   Port-of-Spain   Scarborough

j) What directions would you travel if you sailed from Montego Bay across the Jamaica Channel, through the Windward Passage to the Turks and Caicos Islands?

west, southwest   east, northeast   east, northwest

k) To make a roundtrip from Basseterre (St Kitts and Nevis) to St John's (Antigua and Barbuda), then Montserrat, what directions would you travel?

east, southwest, northwest

east, south

south, southeast, west

6 Using the scale and a ruler, calculate the distance between the following places using the map on pages 10–11 of your *Atlas for Jamaica*. Remember to state your answer to the nearest kilometre.

a) Kingston (Jamaica) and Havana (Cuba)

_____

b) Bridgetown (Barbados) and Port of Spain (Trinidad)

_____

c) Nassau (Bahamas) and Kingston (Jamaica)

_____

d) Castries (St Lucia) and Kingstown (St Vincent)

_____

e) Santo Domingo (Dominican Republic) and San Juan (Puerto Rico)

_____

f) Georgetown (Guyana) and Port of Spain (Trinidad)

_____

g) St John's (Antigua) and Roseau (Dominica)

_____

h) St George's (Grenada) and Castries (St Lucia)

_____

i) Kingston (Jamaica) and George Town (Cayman Islands)

_____

7 **Look at page 7 in the _Atlas for Jamaica_ and read about latitude and longitude. Then, look at the diagram of the Earth and mark on it the following:**

The Equator

The Tropic of Cancer

The Tropic of Capricorn

The North Pole

The South Pole

Northern Hemisphere

Southern Hemisphere

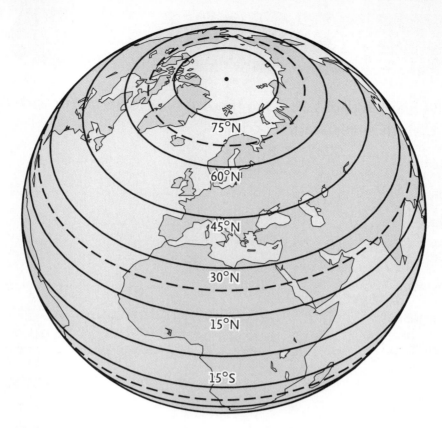

8 Read page 7 in the *Atlas for Jamaica* and circle either true or false for each statement below.

a) Lines of latitude run in an east-west direction.

true false

b) Lines of longitude run in a north-south direction.

true false

c) The Greenwich Meridian is at a longitude of 180°.

true false

d) Lines of longitude run between the North and South Pole.

true false

e) The equator can be used to divide the globe into two halves.

true false

f) The highest number of degrees a line of longitude can be is 180°.

true false

9 **Look at the map on pages 92–93 in the *Atlas for Jamaica*. For each country below, list which hemisphere it occupies.**

a) Australia _____

b) China _____

c) Brazil _____

d) Canada _____

e) Indonesia _____

f) Madagascar _____

g) Jamaica _____

h) Russia _____

I) Poland _____

j) Belize _____

10 **The latitude and longitude for different countries are stated on the next page. Use the world map on pages 92–93 of the *Atlas for Jamaica* to find and circle the error in each statement of latitude and longitude below and then state the correct location for each.**

Tip: Longitude and latitude are measured in degrees, which can be seen at the edges of maps. The diagrams below will help you when you are doing this exercise.

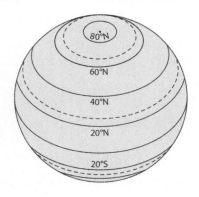

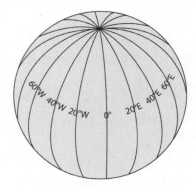

a) Saudi Arabia   20° North, 40° West

Correct location _____

b) Ethiopia   0° West, 40° East

Correct location _____

c) Ecuador   0° South, 60° West

Correct location _____

d) New Zealand   40° South, 120° East

Correct location _____

e) Turkmenistan   40° South, 60° East

Correct location _____

f) Namibia   60° South, 20° East

Correct location _____

11 Use pages 10–13 of the *Atlas for Jamaica* to state the longitude and latitude of the following Caribbean countries and capital cities.

a) Port of Spain, Trinidad _____

b) Grenada _____

c) St Vincent _____

d) Martinique _____

e) Guadeloupe _____

f) St Kitts and Nevis _____

g) Montserrat _____

h) Aruba _____

12 Lines of latitude and longitude are also used to track the location of hurricanes, which are common in the Caribbean between June and November each year. State the Caribbean country that would be threatened if a hurricane were in the following locations below. Use pages 10–11 of your *Atlas for Jamaica* to assist you.

a) 18° North 72° West _____

b) 17° North 61° West _____

c) 13° North 59° West _____

d) 16° North 61° West _____

e) 18° North 77° West _____

f) 25° North 77° West _____

g) 23° North 82° West _____

h) 14° North 61° West _____

13 In 2017, the Caribbean was affected by several hurricanes. One such hurricane was Hurricane Maria, which caused devastation across several Caribbean states. The table below shows the path of Maria over a four-day period. Complete the table by naming one or two countries that would have been threatened by Maria on those dates. Use pages 10–11 of your *Atlas for Jamaica* to assist you.

Date	Latitude	Longitude	Country/Countries threatened
18 September	14.60	62.00	
19 September	16.20	62.80	
20 September	18.90	67.50	
21 September	20.90	70.00	

14 On the map below, plot the location of Hurricane Maria on each date. Insert the date at each location and the names of the different water bodies. Give your map a title and key.

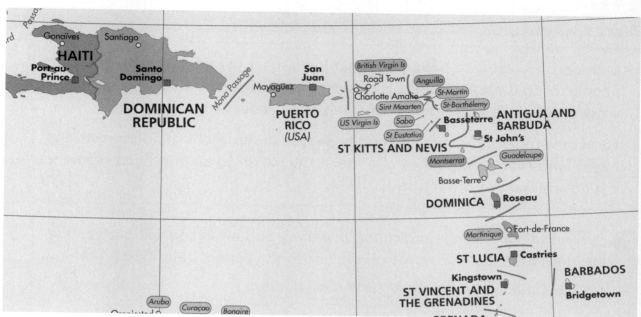

15 Use the information in Exercises 13 and 14, along with your *Atlas for Jamaica*, to answer the questions below.

a) In which water body was Hurricane Maria located on 19 September 2017?

_____

b) Based on the path Maria took, in what direction was the hurricane moving during those four days?

_____

c) On which of the four days was Maria closest to Jamaica?

_____

d) Would you say Maria was moving at a fast or slow rate? Explain.

_____

_____

_____

Grade 5 – Term 2, Unit 3

Each parish in Jamaica has a body that looks after the needs of the parish and people living there. This body is called a *local government*. Local governments work together to share *resources*, *ideas* and *products* through *trade*.

Local governments are *elected* by the people to represent their interests and needs, and even though they operate at the parish level, they must report to the government of the country.

1 Use your *Collins Jamaican School Dictionary* and other sources, such as the internet, to match the words on the left to the correct definition on the right.

a)   An area with its own elected group of people to look after its affairs.

i)   mayor

b)   Concerned with only local matters.

ii)   councillor

c)   A person who has been elected to lead and represent the people of a town.

iii)   regulations

d)   An elected member of a local council.

iv)   local government

e)   Belonging to a city or town that has its own local government.

v)   parish council

f)   Official rules.

vi)   municipal

g)   The group of people who govern the area in which you live.

vii)   parochial

2 Use the internet to research five things your local government or parish council helps to take care of.

_____

_____

_____

_____

_____

3 **Use pages 32–33 and 36–39 of the *Atlas for Jamaica* to complete the map on the next page:**

a) label each parish and its capital

b) list in each box provided for each parish:

    i)   four important products produced

    ii) one physical feature

    iii) one man-made feature

    iv) one historical fact about the parish

c) add a compass rose

d) conduct further research to find out the name of the current Mayor for each parish and add this information to the map on the next page

Grade 5 – Term 3, Unit 1

Weather tells us what the conditions may be on a particular day, while *climate* tells us what type of weather events we are most likely to experience during a particular period of time in the year. It is important to keep track of the weather and climate as they both influence how we live and what we do on a daily basis. A person who studies the weather is called a *meteorologist* and one who studies the climate is called a *climatologist*.

1 Use your *Collins Jamaican School Dictionary* to match each term with its correct definition.

a)   weather

b)   drought

c)   hurricane

d)   storm

e)   climate

     i)   A long period during which there is no rain.

         _____

     ii)   The condition of the atmosphere at any particular time.

         _____

     iii)   The typical weather conditions of a place over an extended period of time.

         _____

     iv)   When there is heavy rain, a strong wind, and often thunder and lightning.

         _____

     v)   A violent wind or storm that usually moves in a circular pattern and affects the Caribbean.

         _____

2   **Use the words given in a) to e) in Exercise 1 to complete the following sentences.**

a)   The _____ report last night said that it will be sunny with gusts of wind, today at 10 am.

b)   _____ change is causing more extreme weather events, such as more violent storms, to occur.

c)   A _____ caused the banana trees to dry up and die, and farmers to lose their earnings.

d)   The _____ season in Jamaica begins in June and ends in November.

e)   High rainfall and high humidity is what happens when a _____ passes by.

3   **For each of the statements below about weather and climate, circle either true or false.**

a)   Weather can change suddenly.

true   false

b)   To determine the climate of a place, data must be collected for many years.

true   false

c)   Jamaica and The Cayman Islands have the same climate, but can have different weather on a particular day.

true   false

d)   To find out if it will be a good day for a picnic tomorrow, you must check the climate.

true   false

e)   The summer months in London are June, July and August. This is an example of the weather in London.

true   false

f)   A change in the climate can cause the weather to change.

true   false

4 Information about the weather and the climate can be shown on maps and graphs. Use the internet to research weather symbols. Complete the table below by drawing symbols you think would best represent the weather conditions listed in the column on the left.

Weather Condition	Weather Symbol
Overcast (95% cloud cover)	
Partly cloudy	
Scattered showers/rain	
Sunny	
Thunderstorm	
High pressure	
Wind direction	

5 Add the symbols in Exercise 4 to the map below to show the weather conditions for the following places in Jamaica. Complete your map with the names of the parishes, a title, compass direction and key.

a) Kingston – mainly sunny, southeasterly winds, temperature 30 °C

b) St Ann – overcast conditions, thunderstorms, northeasterly winds

c) St James – partly cloudy, scattered showers, temperature 24 °C

6 Read pages 34–35 in the *Atlas for Jamaica* and complete the following questions.

a) List the locations, shown on the annual rainfall map of Jamaica, from driest to wettest during the year.

_____

_____

b) What is the difference in rainfall between Mullet Hall in April and Montego Bay in March?

_____

c) How much more rainfall does Port Antonio receive in February, than Kingston in April?

_____

d) What type of climate would you say Jamaica has?

_____

7 **Observe the rainfall and temperature graphs on page 34 and answer the questions below.**

a) Is the temperature the same all year round?

_____

b) Do all places in Jamaica experience the same temperature?

_____

c) What is the highest temperature and the lowest temperature recorded overall?

Highest _____

Lowest _____

d) Does it rain all year round?

_____

e) Which time of the year seems to have the most rain?

_____

f) What conclusion can we draw about the characteristics of the type of climate Jamaica experiences?

_____

_____

_____

_____

_____

8 Farmers depend a lot on rainfall for their crops to grow. Some crops require a lot of rainfall, while other crops do not. Compare the two maps below from *Atlas for Jamaica* to complete the exercise.

Identify the type of crops that can be found growing in each rainfall level.

Average rainfall (mm)	Crop types
>3500	
3000–3500	
2500–3000	
2000–2500	
1500–2000	
1000–1500	
<1000	

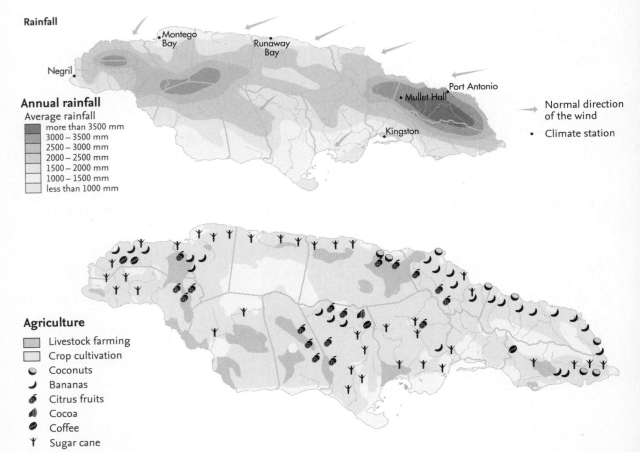

Rainfall

Annual rainfall
Average rainfall
- more than 3500 mm
- 3000 – 3500 mm
- 2500 – 3000 mm
- 2000 – 2500 mm
- 1500 – 2000 mm
- 1000 – 1500 mm
- less than 1000 mm

Montego Bay
Runaway Bay
Negril
Mullet Hall
Port Antonio
Kingston

→ Normal direction of the wind
• Climate station

Agriculture
- Livestock farming
- Crop cultivation
- Coconuts
- Bananas
- Citrus fruits
- Cocoa
- Coffee
- Sugar cane

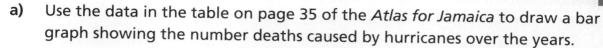

9 **Remember that some weather conditions or events can sometimes be a hazard to us.**

a) Use the data in the table on page 35 of the *Atlas for Jamaica* to draw a bar graph showing the number deaths caused by hurricanes over the years.

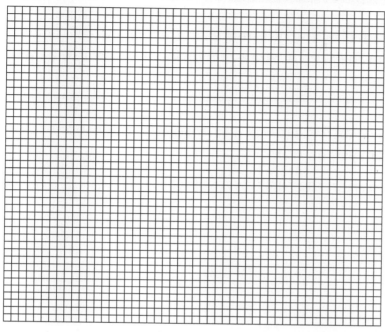

b) In which year was the highest number of deaths recorded?

_____

c) After Hurricane Gilbert, the number of deaths during a hurricane decreased. What do you think contributed to the decline in the number of people dying?

_____

_____

_____

_____

Grade 5 – Term 3, Unit 2

The planets can be arranged by the differences in their characteristics such as size and distance from the Sun. A *three-dimensional model* can help us to visualize these differences.

1 Read pages 8–9 in the *Atlas for Jamaica* and answer the questions to organize the planets of the solar system, from:

a) the closest to the Sun to the furthest away

_____

_____

_____

b) the largest to the smallest

_____

_____

_____

c) the shortest to longest year

_____

_____

_____

d) the longest to shortest day

_____

_____

_____

2 Use your *Collins Jamaican School Dictionary* to write the definitions of each of the following words.

a) planet _____

b) orbit _____

c) solar _____

d) asteroid _____

e) meteor _____

f) comet _____

g) moon _____

h) gravity _____

i) galaxy _____

j) universe _____

3 Use the internet to complete the following questions about our solar system.

a) i) Where in our solar system can the dwarf planet Ceres be found?

_____

ii) What is the diameter of Ceres?

_____

iii) Who discovered Ceres?

_____

iv) When was Ceres discovered?

_____

v) What is the name of the NASA spacecraft that studies Ceres?

_____

G5   The solar system (cont.)

b) What is a solar flare?

_____

_____

c) What is a meteor shower?

_____

_____

d) How long does it take for Halley's comet to return to Earth's vicinity?

_____

e) On which planet can the Great Red Spot be found?

_____

f) On which planet can you find hexagon shaped storms?

_____

g) Which object did the New Horizons spacecraft fly by on 14 July 2015?

_____

h) On which planet can you find the Crommelin Crater?

_____

i) This planet was named after the Roman god of the sea.

_____

j) This planet shares its name with a type of metal.

_____

k) This planet is the brightest planet in the night sky as seen from Earth.

_____

4 Use the internet to do some research and complete the following exercise by matching the fact on the left to the correct planet of our solar system on the right.

a)   This planet is the largest gas giant.

b)   This planet is the smallest in the solar system.

c)   This planet rotates clockwise.

d)   This planet has the coldest atmosphere in the solar system.

e)   This planet is called an ice giant.

f)   This planet has a moon called Titan.

g)   The only planet (other than Earth) that we have successfully explored using robots.

h)   The only planet with complex life.

i)   Mars

ii)   Neptune

iii)   Venus

iv)   Earth

v)   Uranus

vi)   Jupiter

vii) Saturn

viii) Mercury

5 Use the internet to do some research and circle the correct answer from the choices given.

a)   What is the name of the galaxy where Earth is found?

Andromeda   Cantaurus A   Milky Way

b)   Which of the following objects can be found on Earth?

comet   meteorite   asteroid

c)   Which of these objects has a tail?

comet   moon   star

d)   When a meteoroid enters the atmosphere it becomes a:

moon   star   meteor

e)   How many moons does Uranus have?

1   27   18

f)   What was one of the first tools used by people to observe the universe?

telescope   space shuttles   robots

g)   Which of these planets is part of the inner solar system?

Neptune   Jupiter   Venus

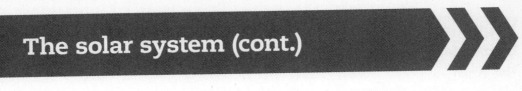

6 **Earth is the only planet in our solar system that can support life.**

a) Take a look back at the diagram on page 8 of your *Atlas for Jamaica*. Why do you think the Earth's location in the solar system allow it to support life?

_____

_____

_____

_____

_____

_____

b) Compare other characteristics of Earth with the other planets. What other features do you think Earth has that allow it to support life?

_____

_____

_____

_____

_____

c) Look at the pictures on pages 22, 23 and 36 in your *Atlas for Jamaica*. What are some of the things that humans continue to do that affect Earth's ability to support life?

_____

_____

_____

_____

_____

7 STEM activity: construct a 3D model of the solar system using pages 8–9 of the *Atlas for Jamaica* as your guide. Use the internet to help research the work.

Your model must show the correct relative sizes of the planets, e.g. Mercury must be much smaller than Jupiter. Your model must also show the correct relative distances of the planets from the Sun, e.g. the distance between the Sun and Earth must be much less than the distance between Earth and Neptune.

Here are some suggestions.

a) You may use styrofoam balls, plasticine/play dough or balls of paper for your planets.

b) You may use cardboard or a piece of wood for your base.

c) You may use wire or pipe cleaners to hold your planets in place.

d) Be creative and use different colours and patterns for your planets.

e) Remember some of the planets have rings. Find a creative way to show the rings.

Reflecting on your task

a) What was the easiest part of making your model?

b) What was the most challenging part?

c) What did you do to help overcome some of the challenges you faced when making your model?

Grade 5 – Term 3, Unit 3

All landscapes are important, and the more we know about them, the better we can protect them and make sure our actions do not harm them. A person who studies different landscapes is called an *ecologist* and a person who studies how we can best use these landscapes without harming them is called an *environmentalist*.

1 Use your *Collins Jamaican School Dictionary* to define each of the following concepts.

a) plants _____

b) environment _____

c) ecology _____

d) habitat _____

e) evergreen _____

f) woodland _____

g) deforestation _____

h) forest _____

i) crop _____

j) pollution _____

2 Use the Caribbean fishing and forestry map on page 18 and the Jamaica landscapes map on page 25, of your *Atlas for Jamaica*, to complete the following questions.

a) Are most of the mangroves (wetlands) in the Caribbean located inland or on the coast?

_____

b) Does the southern or northern side of Haiti have more forest cover?

_____

c) Which two Caribbean countries have the most forest cover?

_____

d) Estimate the percentage of Jamaica that is covered with wetlands.

_____

e) Where is the largest area of forest in Jamaica located?

_____

f) State the three important jobs that Jamaica's wetlands do.

_____

_____

_____

3 Compare the land cover map on page 36 of the *Atlas for Jamaica* with the agriculture map on page 37.

a) What crop is grown closest to the wetland areas?

_____

b) Which crop is most likely to be found growing in the forested areas?

_____

c) Compare the location of livestock farming with the location of wetlands. Why do you think livestock farming occurs close to wetlands?

_____

_____

d) Which product is produced in the Blue Mountains?

_____

4 **Read page 36 of your *Atlas for Jamaica* to complete the questions below.**

a) Based on the pie chart, what was the total percentage of forest cover in Jamaica in 2014?

_____

b) What percentage of forested areas cover in Jamaica in 2014 was protected?

_____

c) What do you think a protected forest area is?

_____

_____

_____

_____

d) What are some of the reasons why deforestation continues to be a major issue in Jamaica?

_____

_____

_____

_____

5 **Use page 36 of your *Atlas for Jamaica* to complete the map.**

a) Shade the forested areas.

b) Shade the wetlands areas.

c) Add a descriptive title to your map, a compass and a key.

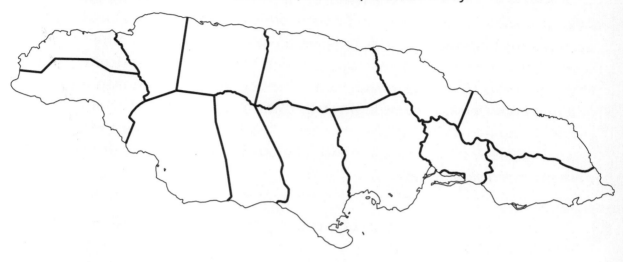

6 **Compare the land cover map on page 36 of the *Atlas for Jamaica* with the industry and minerals map on page 38.**

a) What type of land cover is found at the bauxite mining areas in St Ann parish?

_____

b) What type of land cover is surrounding these bauxite mining areas in St Ann parish?

_____

c) Why is bauxite mining in these areas an issue?

_____

_____

_____

Grade 6 – Term 1, Unit 1

After the *abolition* of slavery and *emancipation*, the freed slaves and their descendants had opportunities to leave the plantation and do other forms of work. This meant that workers were needed to support the agriculture industry. Many migrants from Asia moved to the Caribbean to work on plantations and build new lives. They brought their *culture* with them and over time their culture became part of Caribbean culture. This helped to create a *multicultural region*, where *festivals*, *customs* and *religions* from many parts of the world are now practised side by side.

1 Use the *Collins Jamaican School Dictionary* to write the definition of each of the following words.

a) servant

_____

b) contract

_____

c) festival

_____

d) carnival

_____

e) immigrant

_____

2 Read page 21 of the *Atlas for Jamaica* and complete the map below. Label on the map:

a) The continents, important countries and the areas in China and India where immigrants came from.

b) All of the migration routes to the Caribbean during the 1830s to 1920s.

c) The two bodies of water that immigrants crossed.

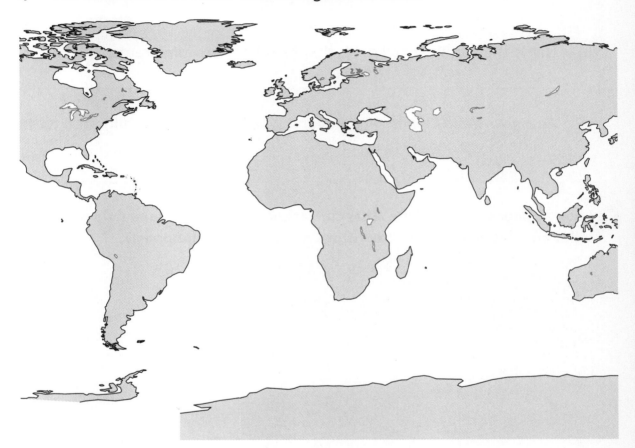

3 Use your *Collins Jamaican School Dictionary* to match the words on the left to the correct definition on the right.

a) culture   i) the possessions or traditions that have been passed from one generation to another

b) heritage   ii) a particular racial or cultural group

c) custom   iii) a traditional activity

d) ethnic   iv) the ideas, customs and art of a particular society

4 Read page 21 of the *Atlas for Jamaica* and answer the questions below.

a) Name the two countries from which the greatest number of people migrated to the Caribbean.

_____

b) Name the Caribbean colonies that recruited the immigrants.

_____

c) Along with the Chinese and Indians, which other groups migrated to the region in the period 1830–1920?

_____

5 Look at pages 88–89 of the *Atlas for Jamaica*. Add to the map below the capital cities and important cities/towns of China, India and Indonesia.

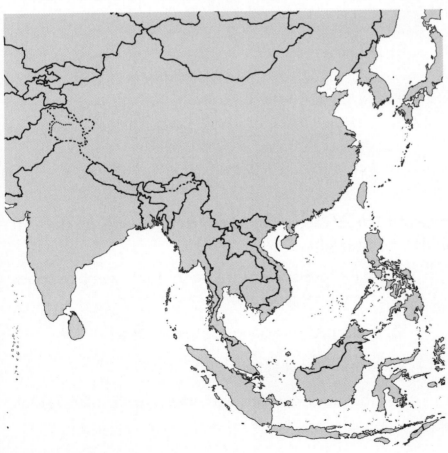

6 **Read pages 88–89 of the *Atlas for Jamaica* to complete the questions below.**

a) Name the desert shared on the Indian and Pakistani border.

_____

b) Name a desert located in China.

_____

c) Complete the names of these Indonesian islands by adding the missing letters.

i) s__m__t__ __

ii) __el__ __ __ s

iii) __ __rne__

iv) n__w g__ i__ __ a

d) Name the body of water found to the:

i) east of India _____

ii) west of India _____

iii) south of India _____

e) Name the body of water found:

i) between China and South Korea _____

ii) between China and the Pacific Ocean _____

iii) to the south of China _____

f) List the four countries that share borders with both India and China.

_____

_____

_____

_____

7 Create a timeline showing the following information about migration to Jamaica.

a) The emancipation of slaves. (1838)

b) The arrival of the first group of Indians to Jamaica. (1845)

c) The arrival of the first group of Chinese to Jamaica. (1854)

d) The arrival of the last group of Indians to Jamaica. (1914)

8 Read page 67 of the *Atlas for Jamaica* about migration to Trinidad and Tobago and add to your timeline the following information.

a) The year in which Indians first arrived in Trinidad and Tobago.

b) The year in which the last group of Indians arrived in Trinidad and Tobago.

c) The year in which the first group of Chinese arrived in Trinidad and Tobago.

d) The years in which groups from Syria and Lebanon arrived in Trinidad and Tobago.

9 **Look at your timeline and answer these questions.**

a) How many years after slavery ended did the first group of Indians arrive in Jamaica to work as indentured servants?

_____

b) How many years after the first group of Indians arrived in Jamaica did the first group of Chinese arrive?

_____

c) Which groups arrived in both Jamaica and Trinidad in the same year?

_____

10 **Use the internet to research the reasons the Indians and Chinese had for migrating to Jamaica. On a separate sheet of paper, design a small poster showing these reasons you have found, and ensure your reasons are clearly classified as push or pull factors.**

G6 — How did Jamaica achieve independence?

Grade 6 – Term 1, Unit 2

In order for the Caribbean to become a more independent region, many changes had to be made. Many great leaders organized and fought for colonial rule to end. They also fought for *voting rights, workers rights* and the *rights of disadvantaged ethnic groups*. This was important so that the decisions made by the government *benefited the majority* and not just the few.

Trade union for workers and *political parties* were formed so that people could *demand change*, as working as a large group was more effective than working as individuals.

1 Use the *Collins Jamaican School Dictionary* to help you match the terms on the left to the correct definition on the right.

a)	colony	**i)**	someone's choice of who they wish to elect in an election
b)	rights	**ii)**	where someone is morally or legally entitled to something
c)	vote	**iii)**	a nation that is not ruled or governed by another country
d)	trade union	**iv)**	an organization of workers that tries to improve the pay and conditions in a particular industry
e)	independent	**v)**	a country controlled by a more powerful country

2 Three significant persons who helped to shape Jamaica's political development and independence were Marcus Garvey, Sir Alexander Bustamante and Norman Manley. Use page 43 of your *Atlas for Jamaica*, and use the internet to do research, to complete the activity below. On a sheet of paper, create a poster showing:

a) The name and a picture of each hero.

b) The date of birth of each hero.

c) Work done by each hero.

3 a) Use the *Collins Jamaican School Dictionary* to help you unscramble the set of words connected with the given term.

independence

r n c t u o y   _____

w n o   _____

s l a w   _____

v o n e g d r e   _____

commonwealth

a t n s o i s a o c i   _____

r w o l d   _____

i t r i a n b   _____

constitution

y s s e t m   _____

g i h t s r   _____

d u e t i s   _____

nation

g r o p u   _____

a s n h r i g   _____

p p e o e l   _____

a l g u n a g e   _____

monarchy

n i k g   _____

e q e u n   _____

g n i e r   _____

franchise

e c e o l i t n   _____

e t v o   _____

g h t r i   _____

revolution

a c e g h n   _____

i v e o l t n   _____

p o i i a l c t l   _____

b) Use your Collins Jamaican School Dictionary and the words from the box to correctly complete the following sentences.

independence	commonwealth	constitution	national
monarchy	franchise	revolutions	

i) The _____ of all countries says that stealing is against the law.

ii) Some enslaved people used violent _____ to free themselves from slavery.

iii) Many countries in the Caribbean gained _____ from Britain in the 20th century.

iv) Queen Elizabeth II is the head of the British _____.

v) Women did not have the _____ in Jamaica before November 20, 1944.

vi) Some _____ countries are still ruled by Britain.

vii) 'Jamaica Land We Love' is the _____ anthem of Jamaica.

4 **Use the information on page 42 of the *Atlas for Jamaica* to draw a timeline in the box provided. This timeline should show:**

a) When slave trade was abolished and the date of emancipation in Jamaica.

b) When Jamaica became a crown colony.

c) When Jamaica gained independence.

d) When major political parties and associations were founded.

e) When Jamaica gained universal adult suffrage.

5 Use the information from the timeline and the information on page 43 of the *Atlas for Jamaica* to answer the questions below.

G6

a) How many years after slavery was each of the three national heroes (Marcus Garvey, Sir Alexander Bustamante and Norman Manley) born?

_____

_____

b) Name one significant event that took place close to when each was born.

_____

_____

c) Explain what was happening in Jamaica at the time when Manley founded the People's National Party.

_____

_____

d) Of the three national heroes, which two played a significant role in Jamaica's independence?

_____

6 Conduct interviews with your parents to find out about the significance of independence and why we celebrate our independence each year on 6 August. Summarize your findings in a short paragraph below.

_____

_____

_____

_____

_____

_____

_____

_____

7 Many countries in the Caribbean achieved their independence at the same time as Jamaica or some years after. There are some countries that are still not independent.

a) Use page 11 in the *Atlas for Jamaica* to complete the table below.

Status	Countries
Independent	
Self-governing	
British Overseas Territory	
Department of France	
Special Municipality	

b) Now draw a bar graph, using the data from the table, showing the number of countries that fall into each of the categories listed in part (a).

8 Use the information on page 11 of the *Atlas for Jamaica* to draw a timeline to show the year of independence of all of the independent countries in the table.

9 Use the data from your table and timeline to answer the following questions.

a) Which country was the first to become independent in the region?

_____

b) Name the country that became independent the same year as Jamaica.

_____

c) Which country was the last to become independent and how many years after Jamaica's independence was this?

_____

d) Is there a larger number of independent territories in the Caribbean than non-independent territories?

_____

10 Look at page 71 of your *Atlas for Jamaica,* and the photo of the celebrations for Republic Day in Guyana. Write a journal entry of about 100 words describing how you and your family celebrate Independence Day in Jamaica. Are there any similarities with Guyana? Use an extra sheet of paper if you need to.

_____

_____

_____

_____

_____

Grade 6 – Term 1, Unit 3

> *National symbols* are a source of *pride* for any nation. They are a great way to remember the *history, culture* and even *landscape* of a country. Any Jamaican, even those living overseas, can recognize Jamaica's national symbols and be reminded of their great nation.

1 Use the *Collins Jamaican School Dictionary* to write the definition of each of the following words.

a) emblem

_____

b) flag

_____

c) symbol

_____

d) nationhood

_____

e) anthem

_____

f) crest

_____

g) motto

_____

2 **Find the ten words hidden in the wordsearch. They may be found vertical, horizontal, diagonal or even backwards.**

emblem	flag	coat-of-arms
nationhood	anthem	crest
motto	patriotism	

symbols
bearing

C	H	H	Y	U	B	K	S	R	F	Z	O	Q	D	U
K	N	V	J	N	P	K	K	G	X	L	N	N	B	Z
O	A	X	B	H	J	N	N	V	Z	M	A	J	Q	R
T	T	N	B	K	T	I	M	K	G	R	F	G	Q	X
T	I	I	S	M	R	A	F	O	T	A	O	C	L	X
O	O	V	D	A	U	X	S	U	F	K	U	B	W	U
M	N	H	E	A	L	L	Q	O	J	J	Q	W	O	W
W	H	B	K	J	O	I	F	V	Y	B	O	V	E	M
H	O	C	L	B	A	Z	Z	D	M	O	B	G	Z	S
E	O	N	M	D	E	M	B	L	E	M	E	B	F	Z
E	D	Y	V	E	B	N	K	C	R	E	S	T	B	L
S	S	R	W	K	V	U	U	J	F	H	A	P	I	Z
H	H	H	S	P	A	T	R	I	O	T	I	S	M	A
G	N	V	Z	U	Q	R	F	D	T	N	M	C	T	W
N	S	L	J	H	K	G	M	O	V	A	L	K	A	Z

3 **Read page 24 of the *Atlas for Jamaica* to complete the questions below.**

a) What does each colour in the Jamaican flag represent?

_____

b) What is the Jamaican motto and where can it be found on the Jamaican Coat of Arms?

_____

c) Explain the meaning of the motto.

_____

d) What does it mean when the pineapple is called an indigenous fruit?

_____

e) The Doctor Bird is native to Jamaica. Is this true or false? Circle the correct answer.

true   false

f) What is the national tree of Jamaica and why is it widely used in reforestation?

_____

g) What is another name for the national flower of Jamaica, the Lignum Vitae plant?

_____

h) Where was the ackee originally from?

_____

i) What do the figures on the Jamaica Coat of Arms represent?

_____

4 You have been given the task to redesign the Jamaican Coat of Arms. In the boxes provided, draw two new symbols you would add to this new design. Say where on the coat of arms you would put them and justify their use by explaining what they would represent.

Symbol 1

Where would it go on the coat of arms?

_____

What does it represent?

_____

Symbol 2

Where would it go on the coat of arms?

_____

What does it represent?

_____

5 Do you know what a protocol is? Use your *Collins Jamaican School Dictionary* to help find its meaning.

Then, use the internet to do further research to find out some of the protocols related to the use of national symbols.

_____

_____

_____

_____

_____

_____

_____

Grade 6 – Term 2, Unit 1

Jamaica has many landforms that are typically seen all over the world, for example nearly half of Jamaica's landscape is over 300 m above sea level. This means there are many important hills, mountains and mountain ranges. Highland areas like these can affect local climate and be used for agriculture and industry and are also important ecosystems.

Mountains and mountain ranges all over the world are well studied, as they are important *physical features* of the natural world.

1 Use the *Collins Jamaican School Dictionary* to write the definition of each of the following words. If any words are not in the dictionary, use the internet to help you.

a) mountain

_____

b) mountain range

_____

c) hill

_____

d) valley

_____

e) plateau

_____

f) landforms

_____

g) plains

_____

h) forest reserve

_____

i) summit

_____

j) slopes

_____

2 Read pages 26–27 of the *Atlas for Jamaica* and complete the names of these Jamaican mountain ranges by adding the missing letters.

a) S_nt_ C_ _z

b) R_ _ H_l_s

c) _ohn _r_ _

d) _ _ue

e) Na_ _ a _

f) M_y D_y

g) Do_ F_ _ue_e_o

h) M_ c_ _

i) _r_ H_ _bo_r

j) Da_l_s

k) l_ _g

l) C_ _k _ _t_ou_t_y

3 Use the clues provided to complete the crossword. Hint: all the answers are from Exercise 1.

Across

1. A natural feature of the Earth's surface
3. A large area of high and fairly flat land
8. Large flat areas of land with very few trees
10. A set of mountains located together

Down

2. An area of trees that is protected by the law
4. A very high piece of land with steep sides
5. A long stretch of land between hills, often with a river flowing through it
6. A rounded area of land higher than the land surrounding it
7. The angle going up the side of a mountain
9. The top of a mountain

4 Use pages 26–27 of the *Atlas for Jamaica* to complete the following on the map.

a) Shade and label the mountain ranges named in Exercise 2.

b) Label the mountain peaks and their heights. Remember a mountain must be over 600 m tall.

c) Insert the names of the parishes.

d) Add an appropriate title to your map, a compass and a key.

Remember that a good map is easy to read, so use sharp coloured pencils to make sure your lines, labels and shading are clean and clear. Ensure that the names of the mountains are correctly placed on the map and that you use an appropriate colour to represent the mountains.

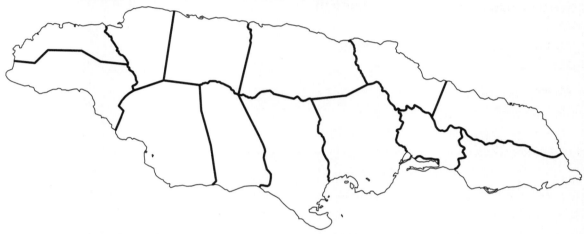

5 Use page 26 in the *Atlas for Jamaica* to list the mountain peaks in Cornwall county from highest to lowest.

Mountain peak	Height	Parish

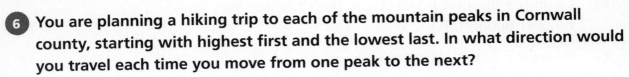

6 You are planning a hiking trip to each of the mountain peaks in Cornwall county, starting with highest first and the lowest last. In what direction would you travel each time you move from one peak to the next?

Use your compass rose and cardinal and inter-cardinal directions to complete the table by stating the directions you would have to travel between each mountain to complete your trip successfully. This first one has been done as an example, to get you started.

Starting mountain	Direction	Ending mountain
Cockpit	South	Malvern
Malvern		

7 Compare the physical map of Jamaica below with the following maps and answer the questions that follow.

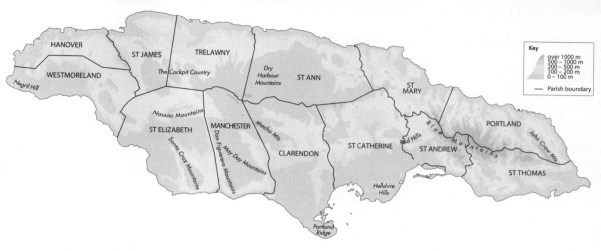

Jamaica climate (page 34)

a) Which mountain range in Jamaica receives the most rainfall?

_____

b) Name one mountain range that receives:

i) 3000–3500 m of rainfall   _____

ii) 2500–3000 m of rainfall   _____

iii) 2000–2500 m of rainfall   _____

Jamaica agriculture (page 37)

c) Are agricultural activities carried out in the mountain ranges of Jamaica?

_____

d) What is the main form of agricultural activities that take place in these areas?

_____

Jamaica industry (page 38)

e) What type of industrial activities do we see taking place in some mountainous areas?

_____

f) Name two mountain ranges and the industrial activity taking place there.

_____

g) What impact do you think these activities might have on the mountain range?

_____

_____

Jamaica tourism (page 44)

h) Mountains are also popular places for different tourist activities. Name some of the points of interest found in Jamaica's mountainous areas. Identify the place and the name of the mountain range.

_____

i) What kind of activities would tourists carry out in mountainous areas?

_____

8 Look at pages 94–95 in the *Atlas for Jamaica* and identify the continent where each of the following mountain ranges is found.

a) Rocky Mountains _____

b) Zagros Mountains _____

c) Ethiopian Highlands _____

d) Andes _____

e) Alps _____

f) Himalaya _____

g) Carpathian Mountains _____

h) Sierra Madre _____

9 Look at pages 94–95 in the *Atlas for Jamaica* and match the peak with the correct height.

a) Mt Whitney   **i)** 5892 m

b) Kilimanjaro   **ii)** 4418 m

c) Mt Kenya   **iii)** 6190 m

d) Mt Everest   **iv)** 5199 m

e) Denali   **v)** 8848 m

10 You will now complete a map showing the major mountain ranges on each of the continents. On the world map below, shade and label the ranges identified in Exercise 8, and insert and label the peaks identified in Exercise 9.

Complete your map with an appropriate title, key and compass rose.

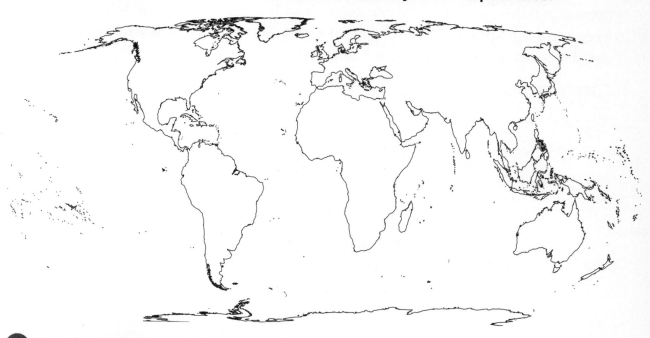

11 Use the internet to help you to write a journal entry outlining what you have discovered about the importance of mountains and what the impact might be if we do not take care of these areas. Use an extra sheet of paper if you need to.

_____

_____

_____

_____

_____

_____

_____

_____

12 **STEM activity: using recyclable materials, design and create a model depicting human activities in a mountainous area and the impact these activities are having on the area. The model should also depict at least one way in which the problems being faced are being dealt with.**

<u>**Criteria for model**</u>

Model should:

– be no more than 18" × 18" in size

– be sturdy and portable

– depict at least two activities carried out in mountainous areas

– depict at least one impact the activities can have on mountainous areas/ features found in mountainous areas

– depict one solution to the problem highlighted

– be made from reusable materials (cardboard, plastic bottles, etc.)

Grade 6 – Term 2, Unit 2

Approximately 71% of the Earth's surface is covered by water. Landmasses such as *continents* and *islands* cover the rest. Bodies of water and landmasses are named differently depending on their shape, size and location.

1 Use the *Collins Jamaican School Dictionary* to write the definition of each of the following words.

a)   continent

_____

b)   island

_____

c)   ocean

_____

d)   sea

_____

e)   lake

_____

f)   river

_____

g)   bay

_____

h)   gulf

_____

i) peninsula

_____

j) isthmus

_____

2 Use pages 94–95 of the *Atlas for Jamaica* and other sources to complete each of the following names below using the words in the box.

HINT: some words are used twice and remember to use the definitions you found to help you.

continent	islands	ocean	sea
lake	bay	gulf	peninsula

a) _____ of Bengal

b) Atlantic _____

c) _____ Victoria

d) Red _____

e) _____ of Mexico

f) Arabian _____

g) Mediterranean _____

h) Southern _____

i) Galapagos _____

j) _____ Superior

3 Use pages 94–95 of the *Atlas for Jamaica* to name the physical feature, landmass or water body found at the following locations.

a) 23.5⁰S 20⁰E _____

b) 20⁰N 60⁰E _____

c) 60⁰N 80⁰W _____

d) 20⁰N 80⁰W _____

4 Use pages 94–95 of the *Atlas for Jamaica* to complete the questions below.

a) Name the continent on which the Kalahari Desert is found.

_____

b) Name the body of water into which the Amazon River flows.

_____

c) Name the continent on which the Great Plains are found.

_____

d) Name the continent on which the Great Victoria Desert is found.

_____

e) Name the continent where Mt Everest is found.

_____

f) Name and state the area of the largest ocean in the world.

_____

g) Name the largest continent and state its area.

_____

h) Name the largest lake and state its area.

_____

i) What is the total area of all the continents?

_____

j) How much larger is North American than South America?

_____

5 Use pages 94–95 of the *Atlas for Jamaica* to help you complete the world map.

a) Label the continents.

b) Shade and label the following deserts and mountain ranges: Sahara, Gobi, Kalahari, Rocky Mountains, Andes, Himalaya.

c) Label the oceans.

d) Label the Caribbean Sea, Mediterranean Sea and South China Sea.

e) Insert the main lines of latitude.

f) Label and write the height of:
Mount Everest, Chimborazo, Mt Whitney, Mt Kenya, Mt Blanc.

g) Shade and label: Lake Huron, Lake Michigan, Lake Superior.

h) Use the internet to locate, shade and label: the Amazon rainforest and the Congo rainforest.

i) Add a compass rose and a key.

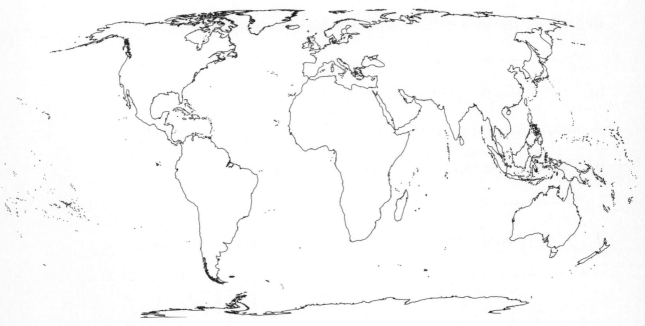

Grade 6 – Term 2, Unit 3

Government has many roles. These include: managing a country's resources and money, keeping law and order and meeting the social needs of its citizens, developing and improving the country and setting up and keeping good relationships with other countries. Government also protects the rights of citizens.

To be effective in doing all of these tasks, government is broken up into departments called *branches*. Each branch has a small part to play and work with each other so that the entire country can meet its goals.

1 Use the *Collins Jamaican School Dictionary* to write the definition of each of the following words.

a) citizen

_____

b) leader

_____

c) democracy

_____

d) cabinet (government)

_____

e) government

_____

f) parliament

_____

g) opposition

_____

h)   senate

_____

i)   monarch

_____

j)   constitution

_____

k)   vote

_____

2 **Every child who is a citizen of Jamaica has the right to an education.**

a) What are some of the things put in place by the government to ensure every child receives an education?

_____

b) Which branch of government would help to protect this right?

_____

3 **Use the internet to research the following:**

a) The names of five government ministries in Jamaica and the names of the minister for each.

_____

_____

_____

_____

b) The names of two senators.

_____

c) The name of the Member of Parliament for the area in which you live.

_____

d) Is the Member of Parliament a part of the government or a member of the opposition?

_____

e) What are some issues facing your community that you would want your Member of Parliament to address?

_____

_____

_____

_____

4 **Use the chart at the bottom of page 24 of the _Atlas for Jamaica_ and other sources to complete the questions below.**

a) Name the three main branches of the Jamaican government.

_____

b) Which branch of the government uses a network of courts to administer the laws of the country?

_____

c) To create a new law, two groups must first discuss and debate the proposed law. Which two groups are these?

_____

d) What is the purpose of the executive?

_____

e) What is another name for the Senate?

_____

f) The House of Representatives is part of which branch of government?

_____

g) The Supreme Court is more powerful than the magistrates court. Is this true or false?

_____

h) Which branch of government controls government finances?

_____

i) How many members are there in Jamaica's Lower House?

_____

j) Who is Jamaica's current Governor-General?

_____

k) Who is Jamaica's current Prime Minister?

_____

l) How many Senators are in Jamaica's government?

_____

5 The Prime Minister works with cabinet members and ministers to carry out the programmes and policies of the government. Why is it important for the Prime Minister to have such a team of persons working with him?

_____

_____

_____

_____

_____

6 Do you think it is a good idea to have the three branches of government separate from each other? Explain your answer.

_____

_____

_____

_____

_____

Grade 6 – Term 3, Unit 1

A *climatic zone* is a broad area on the planet where characteristics such as temperature, rainfall and winds are similar. Studying climatic zones helps us to understand what factors affect climate and how climate in turn affects what we do. We are also better able to understand how what we do can impact the climate and this knowledge also helps us to manage and cope with *climate change*.

1 Use the map on page 96 of the *Atlas for Jamaica* to complete the diagram below.

a) Add labels for the Equator, Tropic of Capricorn, Tropic of Cancer, Arctic Circle, Antarctic Circle.

b) Shade the climatic zones:

    i) ice cap, tundra and mountain, subarctic

    ii) continental, temperate

    iii) subtropical, Mediterranean, semi-arid

c) Add a title, key and a short description for each climatic zone.

2 Use the *Collins Jamaican School Dictionary* and other sources to help to match the terms on the left to the correct definition on the right.

a)   temperature

b)   altitude

c)   latitude

d)   climate

i)   how hot or cold something is

ii)   typical weather conditions in a place

iii)   the height of something above sea level

iv)   the distance of a place north or south of the equator, measured in degrees

3 Use the map on pages 92–93 of your *Atlas for Jamaica* to identify at least two countries found in each climatic zone. Ensure Jamaica is identified.

Climatic Zone	Countries
Tropical	
Temperate	
Polar	

4 Use the map you have completed in Exercise 1, along with other sources such as the internet, complete the following questions by circling the correct answer from each set of choices.

a)   Which climatic zone is found closest to the equator?

   tropical   coastal   polar

b)   Which climatic zone is most likely to have four seasons?

   tropical   polar   temperate

c)   'Cold and dry all year round,' best describes which climatic zone?

   polar   tropical   temperate

d) Which list shows climate zones arranged from driest to wettest?

    i) polar   tropical   temperate

    ii) temperate   polar   tropical

    iii) polar   temperate   tropical

e) Which crop is most likely to grow well in the tropical climatic zone?

    wheat   banana   soybean

f) Which climatic zone do you think is likely the worst for growing crops?

    polar   tropical   temperate

g) Which Caribbean industry do you think is dependent on the climate?

    oil refining   tourism   banking

5 **Use the internet to help complete the questions below. For each of the statements about Caribbean climate, circle either true or false.**

a) The Caribbean is in the tropical climatic zone.

                      true   false

b) The prevailing winds in the Caribbean are the south-east tradewinds.

                      true   false

c) Most Caribbean countries have summer, spring, autumn and winter seasons.

                      true   false

d) A good statement to describe Caribbean climate is:
    'rainy and hot for 6 months, dry and hot for 6 months'.

                      true   false

e) The leeward side of an island in the Caribbean is usually the side of the island facing away from the wind.

                      true   false

f) The leeward side of an island receives more rainfall.

                      true   false

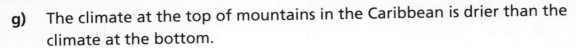

g) The climate at the top of mountains in the Caribbean is drier than the climate at the bottom.

true   false

h) Large Caribbean islands can have more than one type of tropical climate.

true   false

i) Hurricanes sometimes develop over the Caribbean Sea.

true   false

6 Use page 14 of the *Atlas for Jamaica* and the clues provided to complete the crossword.

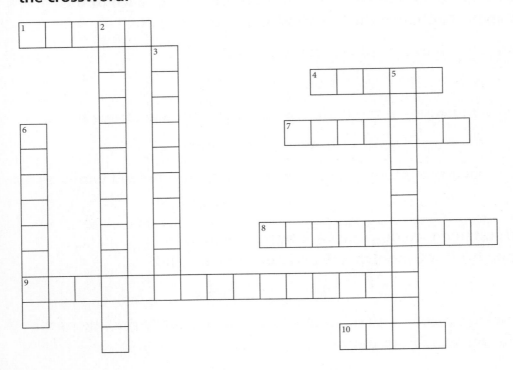

Across
1. The direction of the Gulf Stream as it passes Florida
4. The driest month in Willemstad, Curacao
7. The dominant type of vegetation in Venezuela
8. The direction that the surface winds blow from across the Caribbean
9. The surface current east of the Bahamas
10. The month in which Georgetown, Guyana gets approximately 250 mm of rainfall

Down

2. The dominant climate region in the Caribbean
3. The easternmost climate region in Jamaica
5. The southernmost climate region in the Dominican Republic
6. The northernmost country with a warm temperate climate seen on the map

7 Use the graphs below to complete the table below, and then answer the questions that follow.

City and Country	Wet season (Identify months)	Dry season (Identify months)
Kingston, Jamaica		
Belize City, Belize		
Georgetown, Guyana		
Willemstad, Curacao		
Road Town, British Virgin Is.		

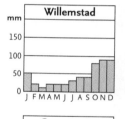

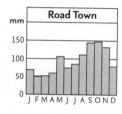

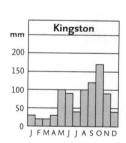

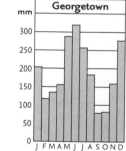

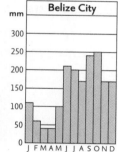

a) Name the country or countries that have more than one wet season.

_____

b) Of the countries, which one has the longest wet period?

_____

c) What is the importance of understanding the wet and dry periods of a country?

_____

_____

_____

8 The climate regions map on page 14 of your *Atlas for Jamaica* shows that even though the Caribbean is found in the tropical zone, each country can still experience different climates.

a) Can you think of two reasons why countries like Jamaica and Haiti have three different climate regions?

_____

_____

_____

_____

b) What are the names of Jamaica's three climate regions?

_____

_____

9 Variation in climate does not only exist in the Caribbean. It happens across the globe. Use the world climate map on page 96 and the world political map on pages 92–93 of the *Atlas for Jamaica* to match the countries on the left to the correct climate type on the right.

a)	Uruguay		i)	tropical
b)	Ukraine		ii)	subarctic
c)	Kyrgyzstan		iii)	mediterranean
d)	Antarctica		iv)	temperate
e)	Egypt		v)	ice cap
f)	New Zealand		vi)	continental
g)	Russia (north)		vii)	semi-arid
h)	Portugal		viii)	desert
i)	Malaysia		ix)	tundra and mountain
j)	Zimbabwe		x)	subtropical

10 Did you know the climate of a place can change? In your own words, explain what you think happens when a climate changes.

_____

_____

_____

_____

_____

11 Use your *Collins Jamaican School Dictionary* to find the word 'extreme', then in your own words, explain what you think an extreme weather event is.

_____

_____

_____

_____

12 In 2017 there were several extreme hurricane events that affected the Caribbean and parts of North America. Take a look at the map and information box on page 15 of your *Atlas for Jamaica* and complete the following:

a) Name three of the hurricanes that affected the region in 2017.

_____

b) How many of these were category 5 hurricanes?

_____

c) Which country was affected by all the hurricanes in 2017 and what was the total number of deaths caused by the hurricanes in that country?

_____

d) i) In which other year was the region affected by three major hurricanes?

_____

ii) Which country was affected by all three, and what was the total number of deaths caused by all three in that country?

_____

13 Apart from severe hurricanes, what other extreme events do you think climate change may cause? Explain your answer.

_____

_____

_____

_____

14 Use the internet to research information about what is causing our climate to change and steps being taken to reduce the effects of climate change. Summarize your findings below.

_____

_____

_____

_____

_____

_____

_____

_____

_____

_____

_____

_____

_____

_____

_____

_____

G6 — The Sun and the Earth

Grade 6 – Term 3, Unit 2

As the Earth *revolves* around the Sun and *rotates* on its *axis*, different parts of the planet are either pointing towards the Sun or away from it. This influences how much sunlight different parts of the Earth receive. Additionally, the length of time that each place receives sunlight also changes. This creates the *seasons* and influences the length of *day* and *night* across the globe.

1 Find the eleven words hidden in the word search puzzle. They may be found vertical, horizontal, diagonal or even backwards.

hemisphere	rotation	revolution	axis
orbit	year	day	sunrise
sunset	equinox	solstice	

I	L	D	P	D	D	C	U	B	S	I	U	R	B	K
N	O	I	T	U	L	O	V	E	R	D	Y	C	Q	E
U	M	R	W	P	E	I	P	Z	D	N	D	O	U	E
J	W	A	M	F	R	N	S	T	E	Y	E	A	R	R
T	I	B	R	O	J	A	I	C	A	C	Q	P	C	Y
N	S	Q	N	F	E	X	I	P	V	V	K	Z	H	R
L	G	L	H	E	M	I	S	P	H	E	R	E	D	M
W	T	S	F	S	N	S	U	O	M	J	C	T	M	S
Z	F	O	A	U	P	U	P	H	H	Y	J	H	Q	W
X	X	L	X	N	H	F	K	B	T	E	X	M	N	Y
I	U	S	C	R	O	T	A	T	I	O	N	M	B	P
Z	V	T	S	I	C	R	G	X	I	Q	M	Y	W	P
W	U	I	D	S	C	Y	T	E	S	N	U	S	F	G
L	K	C	A	E	V	V	O	G	B	A	D	J	K	S
U	Q	E	Y	F	X	O	N	I	U	Q	E	O	Q	I

2 Use the *Collins Jamaican School Dictionary* to write the definition of each of the following words.

a) hemisphere

_____

b) rotation

_____

c) revolution

_____

d) axis

_____

e) orbit

_____

f) year

_____

g) day

_____

h) sunset

_____

i) sunrise

_____

j) equinox

_____

k) solstice

_____

3 Read pages 8–9 of the *Atlas for Jamaica* and information from other sources to complete the following questions.

a) The arrows on the diagram on page 9 indicate the movement of the Earth. What is each type of movement called and what is the difference between the two?

_____

_____

_____

_____

b) Does the Earth rotate clockwise or anticlockwise?

_____

c) Does the Earth revolve around the Sun clockwise or anticlockwise?

_____

d) How long does the Earth take to complete a full rotation on its axis?

_____

e) How long does the Earth take to complete a full revolution around the Sun?

_____

f) Name the direction that the Sun rises in and the direction the Sun sets in.

_____

g) The diagrams illustrating day and night show one half of the Earth in darkness and the other half in light. Explain why it is night-time on one half of the planet, while it is daytime on the other half.

_____

_____

h) What would be the result if the Earth no longer rotated on its axis?

_____

_____

i) Complete the following table.

Day	Date(s)
Summer Solstice in the Northern Hemisphere	
Winter Solstice in the Northern Hemisphere	
Summer Solstice in the Southern Hemisphere	
Winter Solstice in the Southern Hemisphere	
Equinoxes	

j) Complete the following table.

Hemisphere	Season	Months
Northern	Summer	June, July, August
	Autumn	
	Winter	
	Spring	
Southern	Summer	December, January, February
	Autumn	
	Winter	
	Spring	

4 **Complete the diagram below to show the position of the earth on December 21st. Draw and label on your diagram: the direction of sunlight, the north and south poles, the Earth's axis, the equator, the Tropic of Capricorn and the Tropic of Cancer.**

5 **Explain why you think a farmer may:**

a)   plant seedlings in the spring

_____

_____

b)   let the trees grow during the summer

_____

_____

c)   harvest the fruit in the autumn

_____

_____

d)   avoid planting in the winter

_____

_____

6 **Explain why you think a holiday planner may:**

a)   book a seaside hotel during the summer

_____

_____

b)   book a tour to a nature reserve during the spring

_____

_____

c)   plan many tours to the Caribbean from London during the months of
       December to February

_____

_____

7 **STEM activity: construct a 3D model of the revolution of the Earth around the Sun using pages 8 and 9 of the *Atlas for Jamaica* as your guide.**

Your model must clearly show:

– the Sun larger than the Earth

– the Earth tilted on its axis, the north and south poles, the tropics and the equator

– the Earth in the four different positions at the start of each season (you may want to create a static model with the Earth shown at each of the four points shown in the atlas or you may create a moving model with a single Earth that can move around the Sun)

– the correct direction of rotation and revolution of the Earth

Use your creativity and check online for ways to create a moving model or to get the Sun to light up. Remember – always ask an adult for help when doing online research and when constructing your model.

8 **Extended learning:** conduct online and other research to find out how changes in the seasons influence how people dress, design their homes, the foods people eat and recreational activities and jobs they engage in.

Use the box below to capture your findings. Consider using pictures or drawings to enhance your diagram.

Grade 6 – Term 3, Unit 3

The *atmosphere* covers the entire planet and is essential to life. The atmosphere is where we get *oxygen to breathe* and where plants get *carbon dioxide to grow*. It also protects us from some types of *harmful* sunlight. Some human activities can change the atmosphere by creating *pollutants* that enter the air. This is called *air pollution*. Air pollution must be reduced to protect the atmosphere so that it can work well and keep supporting life.

1 Use the *Collins Jamaican School Dictionary* to write the definition of each of the following words.

a) atmosphere

_____

b) ozone layer

_____

c) greenhouse effect

_____

d) global warming

_____

e) acid rain

_____

f) pollution

_____

g) pollutant

_____

2 **Complete each paragraph below using the words in the box for each.**

a)

pollutants	air	dangerous	source

Atmospheric pollution occurs when _____ enter the _____. Human activities can be the _____ of these substances and they have a wide variety of _____ impacts.

b)

vision	asthma	breathing	construction	deforestation

Fine dust created by _____ and mining can blow about and cause difficulty _____. This is especially harmful for people with _____. Pollution by dust can also be an effect of _____, as removing trees makes the soil loose and easy for the wind to pick up. Dust pollution can also reduce _____, as it blocks sunlight and dust can blow into the eyes.

c)

pollution	pesticides	negatively	poisoned	odours

Agriculture can also create air _____. When farmers spray their crops with _____ some of the chemicals create strong _____. People and animals living nearby can be _____ affected by the smell and may even be _____.

d)

build-up	heat	cows	greenhouse	global

Pasture animals such as _____ also create a gas called methane. Methane is a _____ gas. This means it traps _____ close to the Earth's surface. Therefore, when humans raise pasture animals the _____ of methane can contribute to _____ warming.

e)

masks	fossil	factories	weather

Burning _____ fuels in car engines and _____ can also pollute the atmosphere. Smog is created in this way. Some cities are so covered with smog that the people have to wear _____ and the smog can even change the _____.

3 **Read page 100 in the *Atlas for Jamaica*.**

a) Add labels to the diagram below.

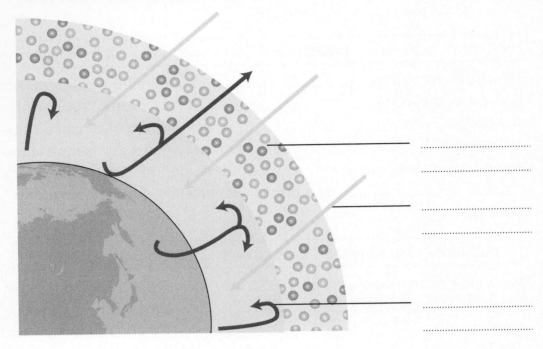

b) Answer the following questions.

i) Where do greenhouse gases build up?

_____

_____

ii) What would the temperature be on Earth without greenhouse gases?

_____

_____

iii) What do greenhouse gases do?

_____

_____

4 Use the internet, and pages 100–101 of the *Atlas for Jamaica*, to research the effects of air pollution on Los Angeles and Tokyo. Complete the fact file below.

Los Angeles

a) Name of the country in which it is found.

_____

b) What is the city's population?

_____

c) List the top three economic activities in the city.

_____

d) List two sources of air pollution in the city and name the pollutants.

_____

e) Describe one way the city has tried to reduce air pollution.

_____

Tokyo

a) Name country in which it is found.

_____

b) What is the city's population?

_____

c) List the top three economic activities in the city.

_____

d) List two sources of air pollution in the city and name the pollutants.

_____

e) Describe one way the city has tried to reduce air pollution.

_____

5 Industrial activities are major contributors to air pollution. Look at page 38 of the *Atlas for Jamaica* and answer the following questions.

a) List the different industrial activities on the map that would contribute in some ways to atmospheric pollution.

_____

_____

b) Which parish or region is likely to have the highest level of atmospheric pollution? Justify your answer with evidence from the map.

_____

_____

c) If Jamaica were to stop these industrial activities so that atmospheric pollution is reduced, what impact do you think this would have on society?

_____

_____

d) Do you think it is possible to have a balance between industrial activities and protecting the atmosphere? Justify your answer.

_____

_____

Grade 6 – Term 3, Unit 4

The Caribbean is a small region, and the countries that are a part of it are even smaller. This means that working together and *sharing resources and ideas* is important for reaching larger goals that each country may not be able to reach on its own. This is the role of *regional organisations*. Regional organisations are set up so that each country can *benefit from unity* in the areas of trade, business, health, sports and education. This also allows the region to be more *powerful* on the world stage.

1 Use the *Collins Jamaican School Dictionary* and other sources to write the definition of each of the following words.

a) neighbour

_____

b) cooperation

_____

c) region

_____

d) integration

_____

e) organisation

_____

f) bilateral

_____

2 Match the organisation to their function.

a) Caribbean Community (CARICOM)

b) Caribbean Free Trade Association (CARIFTA)

c) Organisation of Eastern Caribbean States (OECS)

i) To promote economic integration, and protecting human and legal rights.

ii) To improve living standards, promote economic integration and cooperation, and coordinate foreign policy.

iii) To encourage balanced development in the region by increasing and diversifying trade.

3 Use the information on page 45 of the *Atlas for Jamaica* and from the internet to draw a timeline to show:

a) the creation and end of the West Indies Federation

b) the creation of the Caribbean Community (CARICOM)

c) the creation of the Caribbean Free Trade Association (CARIFTA)

d) the creation of the Organisation of Eastern Caribbean States (OECS)

e) the date Jamaica exited the West Indies Federation

f) the date of independence for Jamaica and Barbados

g) the creation of:

    i) Caribbean Court of Justice (CCJ)

    ii) University of West Indies (UWI)

    iii) Caribbean Examinations Council (CXC)

    iv) Caribbean Disaster Emergency Management Agency (CDEMA)

    v) Caribbean Public Health Agency (CARPHA)

    vi) West Indies Cricket Board (WICB)

4 a) Use pages 46–72 of the Caribbean section of the *Atlas for Jamaica* and the internet to complete the table below.

Country	Main economic activity	Main export	Main import	Main export partner	Main import partner
Antigua and Barbuda					
Bahamas					
Barbados					
Belize					
Dominica					
Grenada					
Guyana					
Haiti					
Jamaica					
Montserrat					
St Kitts & Nevis					
St Lucia					
St Vincent and the Grenadines					
Suriname					
Trinidad and Tobago					

b) Examine the information in the table above, and then write a summary of some of the similarities and differences among CARICOM member states.

_____

_____

_____

_____

_____

_____

_____

_____

5 Use the internet to research the regional organisations listed below. For each organization, state its full name, two of its functions and its current chairperson or head.

CARICOM

_____

_____

_____

Caribbean Disaster Emergency Management Agency (CDEMA)

_____

_____

_____

Caribbean Court of Justice (CCJ)

_____

_____

_____

University of West Indies (UWI)

_____

_____

_____

6 What conclusion can you draw about the benefits of regional integration based on the functions of the different organisations above?

_____

_____

_____

_____

Index